Columbia University

Contributions to Education

Teachers College Series

No. 393

AMS PRESS

NEW YORK

A PERSONNEL STUDY OF DEANS OF GIRLS IN HIGH SCHOOLS

By

SARAH M. STURTEVANT, A.M.
ASSOCIATE PROFESSOR OF EDUCATION
TEACHERS COLLEGE, COLUMBIA UNIVERSITY

AND

RUTH STRANG, Ph.D. 144528
ASSISTANT PROFESSOR OF EDUCATION
TEACHERS COLLEGE, COLUMBIA UNIVERSITY

TEACHERS COLLEGE, COLUMBIA UNIVERSITY
CONTRIBUTIONS TO EDUCATION, NO. 393

BUREAU OF PUBLICATIONS
Teachers College, Columbia University
NEW YORK CITY
1929

Library of Congress Cataloging in Publication Data

Sturtevant, Sarah Martha, 1881-1942.
   A personnel study of deans of girls in high schools.

   Reprint of the 1929 ed., issued in series: Teachers
College, Columbia University. Contributions to
education, no. 393.
   1. Deans of women--United States. 2. High
schools--United States. I. Strang, Ruth May, 1895-
joint author. II. Title. III. Series: Columbia
University. Teachers College. Contributions to
education, no. 393.
LB1620.5.S75 1972   373.1'2'01   71-177730
ISBN 0-404-55393-1

Reprinted by Special Arrangement with Teachers
College Press, New York, New York

From the edition of 1929, New York
First AMS edition published in 1972
Manufactured in the United States

AMS PRESS, INC.
NEW YORK, N. Y.   10003

FOREWORD

The purpose of this study is to give a more recent and comprehensive view of the status and function of deans of girls in secondary schools than any which has previously been made. It is a companion study to the two monographs already published by Teachers College, one by Jones [1] concerning the women deans in colleges and universities, and the other by the authors of the present study relating to the status and function of deans of women in teachers colleges and normal schools.[2] In order to study the "best" practice rather than the "average" practice, one hundred deans were selected for the survey rather than a random sampling of deans throughout the country. The inquiry was undertaken by the department of Advisers of Women and Girls, Teachers College, Columbia University, with the essential assistance of deans of girls in secondary schools in various parts of the United States. The interest has been so genuine and the information so carefully given that it may well be called a cooperative study. Grateful acknowledgment is made to these deans and to Miss Sadie B. Campbell, Dean of Girls in North High School, Des Moines, Iowa and Felix Warburg-fellow in the Education of Women and Girls in 1928, for her valuable assistance in tabulating and interpreting the material.

The inquiry is divided into eleven parts. Chapter I gives a general description of the study, states the specific questions to be answered, describes the group selected for study, and outlines the methods used in the investigation. Chapter II deals with four aspects of the position,—the number of schools having a woman officially appointed to supervise the various phases of school life of the girls, the titles used, the ranks held, and the method of appointment to the position. Chapter III describes the academic, administrative, and social experience, and the educational his-

[1] Jones, Jane Louise, *A Personnel Study of Women Deans in Colleges and Universities*, Bureau of Publications, Teachers College, Columbia University, 1929.

[2] Sturtevant and Strang, *A Personnel Study of Deans of Women in Teachers Colleges and Normal Schools*, Bureau of Publications, Teachers College, Columbia University, 1928.

tory of these deans. Chapter IV contains data concerning the salary of deans of girls, and some factors influencing salary.

Chapter V consists of a summary of the duties which the majority of these deans perform—those which they think they should perform, and those to which they devote the largest amount of their time. Chapter VI is a detailed study of each phase of the dean's work. Chapter VII deals with the important topic of the dean's relationships with the principal, home-room teachers, class advisers, club sponsors, pupils, parents and outside agencies, and her work on committees.

Chapter VIII, a case study of the dean's work in one school, adds vividness to the statistical treatment of the data from the one hundred deans. Chapter IX consists of opinions of deans regarding the professional satisfactions and problems of the position. Chapter X combines a brief summary with an evaluation of some of the most significant findings of the investigation.

Chapter XI is a summary of a similar study of the deans of girls in high schools in New York State enrolling more than one hundred and fifty pupils.

CONTENTS

TABLES

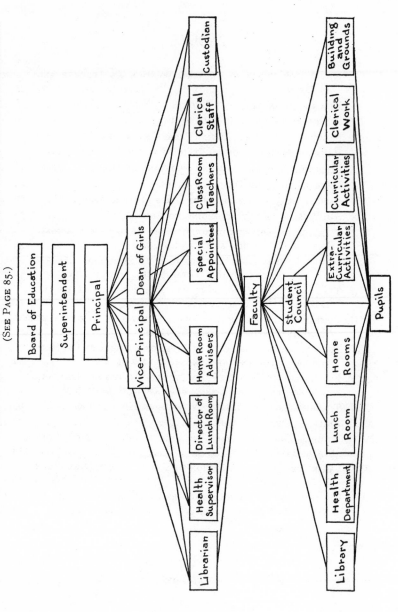

CHART I. RELATIONSHIP OF DEAN TO ORGANIZATION AS A WHOLE IN ONE HIGH SCHOOL TAKEN AS A CASE STUDY
(SEE PAGE 85.)

Board of Education

Superintendent

Principal

Vice-Principal | Dean of Girls

Librarian — Health Supervisor — Director of Lunch Room — Home Room Advisers — Special Appointees — Class Room Teachers — Clerical Staff — Custodian

Faculty

Student Council

Library — Health Department — Lunch Room — Home Rooms — Extra-Curricular Activities — Curricular Activities — Clerical Work — Building and Grounds

Pupils

CHAPTER I

PROBLEMS AND METHODS

In the United States there are 17,710 high schools enrolling 3,065,009 pupils [1] all of whom, according to best educational theory, must be dealt with as individuals and developed in the social attitudes of good citizens as well as inducted into the learning of the ages. The personnel and equipment of the modern school has been modified and expanded to take care of the new demands upon it. Visiting teachers, vocational counsellors, health experts, deans of girls, and other specialists have in many cases been added to the staff of the high school.

Not the least important among these new types of service offered in the high school is the contribution made through the office of dean of girls.

It may be estimated from a sampling of seven states that at this time one-fourth to one-third of high schools enrolling more than one hundred and fifty pupils employ a woman, usually called *Dean of Girls,* who is officially appointed to supervise the school life of all the girls. Frequent inquiries among deans and principals concerning the status and function of this office indicate the need for more recent, more detailed, more extensive, and more representative investigation, than has yet been made of the best practice in regard to this vocation. In order to supplement the excellent published and unpublished studies already available, an investigation was undertaken in the fall of 1928, and is here reported.

General Description of the Investigation

The difficulties involved in making a complete study of the office of the dean in high schools, such as was made by Jones [2] of woman deans in colleges and universities, and by Sturtevant and

[1] *Biennial Survey of Education Bulletin,* 1928, No. 25, p. 1047. Bureau of Education, Department of the Interior, Washington, D. C.

[2] Jones. Jane Louise, *A Personnel Study of Women Deans in Colleges and Universities,* New York City, Teachers College, Bureau of Publications, 1928.

Strang [3] of deans of women in teacher training institutions were so great, that it seemed unwise to attempt it. In the first place an effort to reach by questionnaire every high school in the United States would entail an expenditure in time and money unwarranted by the results which would probably be obtained. In the second place, there is still, in spite of nearly twenty years of its use, in many quarters so very little understanding of what the title "dean of girls" connotes that there was little hope of getting a complete and bona fide list of deans of girls. Sometimes a Girl Reserve club leader is given the title, or a vice-principal, as physical education director, or some other official who has little in common in terms of function. Again, persons performing similar duties are denoted by various titles such as "dean of girls," "adviser of girls," "counselor," or any one of several others. Accordingly, schools which in fact have women performing the function of the dean of girls might not be listed as having such a member of their faculties if the term "dean of girls" were used in the inquiry. This confusion in nomenclature and the consequent unreliability of data obtained made it seem that an attempt at a study of the whole field would be unprofitable at this time.

In the third place, it seemed that in view of requests from deans and principals for information concerning the approved status and the particular functions of this office, it would be more profitable to make an intensive study of a carefully selected group of deans than to duplicate the method or scope of the previous studies.

A Recent Study. The present study is needed to furnish current information concerning the items investigated in earlier studies, to obtain a more exact idea of the prevalence of the office of dean of girls and to supplement Good's excellent recent study (1927) [4] by obtaining more detailed information concerning the duties of deans and by investigating a different group of schools.*

A Detailed Study. In this survey, as in previous investigations, information concerning salary, teaching experience, educational

[3] Sturtevant, Sarah M. and Strang, Ruth, *A Personnel Study of Deans of Women in Teachers Colleges and Normal Schools,* New York City, Bureau of Publications, Teachers College, Columbia University, 1928.

[4] Good, Virginia and Good, Carter V., "A Study of the Dean of Girls in Secondary Schools," *Educational Administration and Supervision,* 13:599-610, December 1927.

* Only eight high schools contributing to the study by Good were included in this investigation.

history, and rank was obtained. The duties, however, were analyzed into more specific performance items. Instead of merely asking whether a dozen general duties were performed by the dean, the questionnaire used in this study listed eighty-eight specific duties. Concerning each of these duties four questions were asked: Is the duty performed in the school? Is it performed by the dean? Is it performed by others? Should the dean assume responsibility for this duty either alone or in coöperation with other members of the staff? Several additional questions were included to ascertain the duties which demand the largest amount of the dean's time, the part of her work which has been commented on favorably, and the part which has received unfavorable criticism. It is especially in the analysis of duties that this report makes a more detailed contribution to the understanding of the position of dean of girls than do previous studies.

An Extensive Study. In addition to the hundred selected deans, similar surveys are being made of all high schools enrolling one hundred fifty or more pupils in a number of states—New York, North Carolina, New Jersey, Kansas, Iowa, Indiana, and Oklahoma. These will be published from time to time, probably in the state journals, and will furnish an interesting basis for comparison of the position of dean of girls in different parts of the country.

METHOD OF STUDY

A combination of four methods was used in obtaining the data for this study: The questionnaire, the time schedule, observation, and case study. A description of each follows.

The Questionnaire. In order to ascertain the number of deans of girls in high schools of the country, questionnaires were sent, in coöperation with individuals or with state deans' associations, to the principals of all the high schools enrolling one hundred and fifty or more pupils in seven states. These questionnaires asked if there were in the school a "woman OFFICIALLY APPOINTED to supervise the various phases of school life among the girls" and for her name if there were such a person. From these states there was a 90 to 100 per cent return.

In order to make a study representative of the best practice, a second, detailed questionnaire, thirteen pages in length, was sent to one hundred deans from thirty-two states who were selected

on the basis of their experience, professional training, membership in the national and state associations of deans, or their outstanding contributions. From these there was a 100 per cent
return.

In order to get a complete picture of the deans in a given
section, the long questionnaire was sent to all the women reported
by the principals of New York State high schools as having been
OFFICIALLY APPOINTED to supervise the various phases of school
life among the girls. Fifty-seven, or 68 per cent, of these women
replied.

The three main objections to the questionnaire as a method of
obtaining information were partly overcome in this study. In
the first place, because replies were received from all of the
one hundred deans selected, the problem of adequacy of sampling
did not arise. Similarly, percentage of returns from the other
groups was very large. In the second place, the questionnaires were
carefully tested and criticized before being sent out, and ambig-
uous questions practically eliminated. In the third place, the co-
operation of the deans was secured to an unusual extent. Frequently the answered questionnaire was returned with statements
such as the following: "I assure you that I gladly filled out the
questionnaire"; "I found the filling out of the questionnaire most
helpful, since it gave me suggestions of opportunities for service
which I had never considered"; "I am sending by this same mail
the questionnaire, all filled out, and all filled out means some-
thing in this case, does it not? It is a valuable undertaking and
I am glad to do my part in it."

Information was obtained from the questionnaires which could
not have been secured in any other way from so large a group
scattered throughout the United States.

The Daily Schedule. Twenty-one deans generously agreed to
keep a daily record for two weeks of their activities during their
professional day. Ideally, schedules should be kept during an
entire year since there are seasonal variations in the dean's work,
but such a task is obviously impossible. The two weeks were
chosen near the middle of the term to avoid the special duties of
the beginning and the end of the year. The activities were immediately recorded during the day—not summarized from memory at
the end of the day. Each schedule gives a clear picture of the

dean at work—"a photograph which her friends would recognize." These twenty schedules were summarized into what Williston describes as a job specification—"a composite of the records of performance of *several different* individuals who did the same job. It describes the essential activities of all individuals who do this job. It eliminates from records of performance nonessential personal peculiarities characteristic of any particular individual's work." [5]

The questionnaire shows the number of deans who perform a given duty; the time schedules show the amount of time spent each day in performing each duty.

Observation. Visits were made to five schools, in which the dean permitted the observer to sit in her office for a day, observing

TABLE I

NUMBER OF YEARS IN PRESENT POSITION AS TEACHER AND AS DEAN

(100 Selected Deans)

	NUMBER OF CASES	LOWEST	MEAN	HIGHEST	S.D.
Experience as teacher					
Group I*	12	1	6.46	15	
Group II	29	0	5.26	22	
Group III	31	0	3.24	18	
Group IV	28	0	8.27	26	
Total (All groups)	100	0	5.62	26	6.56
Experience as dean					
Group I	12	⅓	3.32	13	
Group II	29	1	4.62	13	
Group III	31	1	4.39	13	
Group IV	28	½	7.13	17	
Total (All groups)	100	⅓	5.09	17	3.58

This table should be read as follows: In the 12 schools in Group I—those enrolling from 250 to 499 pupils—the smallest number of years of experience as teacher which any dean has had is 1; the average is 6.46; the largest number of years is 15; etc.

* For explanation of Groups see page 8.

[5] Williston, Arthur L., "Activities of Research Scientist," *The Educational Record,* X:126-131, April, 1929.

and recording her activities, and interviewing her when she was not busy with other people. While the questionnaire shows merely that the duty was performed, and the daily schedule contributes quantitative data, observation reveals qualitative aspects which are not obtained by the other methods. Further study of each duty demands intensive observation. In this survey the visits are used as an incidental aid in interpreting the data obtained by the other methods and in writing the case studies of two high schools.

The Case Study. To the above methods was added an intensive study of one school in order to give a clear and vivid picture of a dean at work in a practical situatipn.

SELECTION OF THE GROUPS TO BE STUDIED

A. STATE GROUPS

Several factors entered into the selection of the states which were studied to determine the number of deans of girls which they have in their high schools. These factors included geographical distribution, development of state associations of deans, and available coöperation from those associations in a study of the situation in their own states.

The New York State Association of Deans undertook also the more intensive investigation which is here included to show the work of deans in a given area.

B. ONE HUNDRED SELECTED DEANS

Since the aim of this investigation was primarily to study deans who are representative of the best, rather than the average, or mediocre, practice, a group of one hundred deans were selected rather than taken at random from among deans in the United States.

One Basis of Selection—Experience as Dean. All but three of the deans chosen have had at least one year of experience as a bona fide dean in their present situations and are so recognized by title and status; 89 have served as dean two or more years; 59, four years or longer; 32, at least six years; and 13, ten or more years. The median number of years of experience as dean is 4.7. Table I shows the mean and range in experience of this group as teacher and as dean in the schools in which they are at present located.

In a period of service such as this, the needs of pupils could be studied, coöperation with faculty secured, methods and procedures evolved, essential duties given their proper places, and group projects and programs initiated and put into operation. In other words, these women have served as deans long enough to have obtained an insight into the needs and possibilities of the position.

A Second Basis of Selection—Professional Interest. One indication of professional aliveness is active membership in national, city, or state associations of deans. Of the one hundred deans studied, at least sixty-two are members of the National Association of Deans of Women. In conferences of professional people, deans gain information, inspiration, and encouragement both from the speakers and from contacts with fellow deans.

Another indication of professional interest is advanced study in the field. Four-fifths of this group have taken a professional course in advisory work. Although training does not guarantee success, it should give a broader view of the position and more knowledge and skill in performing specific phases of the work.

A Third Basis of Selection—Evidence of Good Work. In the case of most of these hundred deans, some evidence of the effectiveness of their work was obtained through voluntary comments of principals or other people familiar with the schools; through visits to the schools which revealed the dean's influence indirectly by the attitudes of pupils and the activities in which they were engaging; and through speeches or articles which the deans have made or written.

On these three bases the one hundred deans were selected. There are many other deans doing effective advisory work who might well have been included in the study, but practical difficulties in tabulating replies made it necessary to limit the number to one hundred.

Description of the Schools Included in the Study. Tables II and III show that the schools from which the one hundred deans were selected represent a wide range of size and geographical location. Because significant differences in some respects may be found in schools of different sizes, the data were tabulated as follows:

Group I   —Schools having a total enrollment of 250-499 pupils.

Group II   —Schools having a total enrollment of 500-999 pupils.

Group III —Schools having a total enrollment of more than 1000 pupils, but less than 1000 girls.

Group IV —Schools having a total enrollment of more than 1000 girls.

In general the number of boys and girls in these high schools is almost equal and the results of other studies which are classified according to the enrollment of girls may easily be compared with this study.

TABLE II

DESCRIPTION OF THE FOUR GROUPS OF SCHOOLS

(*100 Selected Deans*)

	GROUP I	GROUP II	GROUP III	GROUP IV	TOTAL
Number of cases	12	29	31	28	100
Total enrollment Range .... Mean	250–463 321	507–957 737	1018–1926 1368	1685–6200 2751	250–6200 1419
Enrollment of girls Range .... Mean	130–273 183	257–542 389	559–963 711	1012–5000 1563	130–5000 793
Mean ratio of teachers to pupils	19	21	23	26	23

This table is read as follows: In the 12 schools in Group I, the total enrollment ranges from 250-463 pupils; the mean being 321. The enrollment of girls ranges from 130 to 273, the mean being 183. There is one teacher to every 19 pupils, etc.

STATEMENT OF THE PROBLEM

Objective data have been obtained which will answer to some extent two groups of questions: (1) those relating to the number of schools having deans of girls, their titles, rank, method of appointment, experience and training, staff and equipment, and the salary they receive; (2) those relating to the duties of the deans of girls, their relationships to other members of the faculty, and the special problems of their office.

TABLE III

STATES REPRESENTED IN THIS STUDY

NAME OF STATE	NUMBER OF SCHOOLS	NAME OF STATE	NUMBER OF SCHOOLS
Alabama	1	Montana	3
Arizona	1	Nebraska	3
California	12	New Hampshire	2
Colorado	3	New Jersey	5
Connecticut	3	New York	7
Delaware	1	North Carolina	5
Florida	1	Ohio	5
Illinois	6	Oklahoma	2
Indiana	3	Oregon	2
Iowa	3	Pennsylvania	7
Kansas	1	Rhode Island	2
Kentucky	1	South Dakota	1
Maine	1	Texas	1
Massachusetts	3	Washington	2
Michigan	4	West Virginia	1
Minnesota	3	Wisconsin	3
Missouri	2		

Questions relating to the number of deans:

How many high schools have a woman officially appointed to supervise the school life of all the girls?

How long have these deans been in their present position?

Questions relating to the title and rank of deans:

What titles do these women hold?

What titles are most satisfactory to them?

What rank in the school is equivalent to the dean's?

Questions relating to method of appointment:

Are deans usually selected from the faculty of the school to which they are appointed?

Is their salary increased to parallel their new responsibility?

What is the average amount of increase of salary?

Questions relating to experience and training:

What degrees and diplomas do deans hold?

By what professional route have they reached their position as dean?

How many have taken a professional course in advisory work?

What part of their academic and professional training and professional and life experiences has contributed most to their success as dean?

Have they felt a need of any specific knowledge and techniques?

Questions relating to staff and equipment:

Do deans have private offices?

What equipment do they have?

What equipment would they like to have?

How much assistance do deans have in their work?

Questions relating to salary:

What is the range, and the average salary of deans?

How does the dean's salary compare with that of teachers and principals in high schools?

Questions relating to duties:

What duties do the majority of deans perform, alone or in co-operation with others?

What duties do deans think they should perform?

What duties take the largest amount of the dean's time?

How many of the duties which the present situation demands of them do they think should be delegated to some one else?

On which committees do they serve?

What part of their work has received favorable comments?

What part has been subject to criticism?

In which phases of the work do deans feel they have accomplished most? In which phases, least?

How many hours a week do deans teach?

Is night work necessary? If so, of what kind?

Other questions:

What is the working relation of deans to other members of the staff? to parents? to pupils? to outside agencies?

What do deans consider the main professional satisfactions; the chief difficulties, and problems of their positions?

VALUE OF THE INVESTIGATION

This study should be helpful to teachers interested in the work of dean of girls, to principals contemplating the establishment of the office in their schools, to deans in service eager to know the status and function of deans in other schools, and to instructors giving professional courses for deans.

CHAPTER II

THE POSITION OF DEAN OF GIRLS

Four aspects of the position of Dean of Girls will be discussed in this chapter: The prevalence of the position, and the title, rank, and method of appointment of the dean.

INSTITUTIONS HAVING DEANS OF GIRLS

How many secondary schools in the United States have established the office of Dean of Girls? Since the study of the one hundred selected deans does not answer this question, the results of previous surveys and of some of the unpublished recent state studies will be presented.

The data relating to this question in previous studies are unreliable because of the low percentage of replies to the questionnaires. There is no way of knowing whether or not the schools which did not reply have deans. From experience with follow-up letters, there is some evidence that the majority of schools which do not reply are the ones which have no deans. The percentage of schools having deans, therefore, is undoubtedly lower than the figures given in Tables IV. In some of the recent state studies the results are more reliable because replies were received from approximately one hundred per cent of the principals of all the schools having an enrollment of one hundred and fifty or more pupils.

Another factor which makes the true percentage of schools having deans lower than the reported percentages is the discrepancy between the title given and the real status of the person called by that title. In New York State, for example, 83 principals reported that they had deans of girls, but only 65 of these persons designated as dean were actually serving in that capacity according to their own statements.

Table IV shows the percentage of schools having deans. Some of the 1928 state studies as well as the more general previous studies are included in this summary. It will be noted that in four of the recent state studies made under the direction of the department of Advisers of Women, Teachers College, Columbia University, approximately one-third of the high schools enrolling

TABLE IV

NUMBER OF SCHOOLS HAVING DEANS

(*Summary of Studies*)

	NUMBER OF QUESTION-NAIRES SENT	QUESTIONNAIRES RETURNED		SCHOOLS REPORTING DEANS OF GIRLS*	
		Number	Per Cent	Number	Per Cent
State studies—1928					
New York State ...	257	257	100	83	32
Kansas[a]	120	116	97	40	34
North Carolina[b] ...	146	144	99	53	37
Iowa[c]	162	148	91	56	38
California[d]	312	282	90	137	49
Indiana[e]	163	157	96	102	63
Oklahoma[f]	133	133	100	59	44
Previous studies					
Stevens (original study, 1917)	92	89	97	54	61
Barker (1922)	500	278	56	139	50
Sturtevant (1923) ..	317	159	50	106	67
Good (1927)	300	177	59	104	59
Switzer (1928)[g] ...	887	552	62	329	60

With the exception of California, these state studies were made under the direction of the department of Advisers of Woman, Teachers College, Columbia University, and with the coöperation of the State Deans' Associations in Iowa, New York, Indiana, and North Carolina working through their research committees.

* These figures indicate the number of principals who reported that they had a woman officially appointed to supervise the various phases of the school life for all the girls.

[a] D. A. Kinniburgh, *Deans of Girls in High Schools of Kansas*. Unpublished report, 1928.

[b] Fannie S. Mitchell, *Deans of Girls in High Schools of North Carolina*. Unpublished study, 1928.

[c] Iowa State Deans' Association, *Deans of Girls in High Schools in Iowa*. Unpublished study, 1929.

[d] Opal R. Switzer, *Deans of Girls in Senior High Schools in California*. Unpublished study, 1928.

[e] Indiana State Deans' Association, *Deans of Girls in Junior and Senior High Schools in Indiana*. Unpublished study, 1929.

[f] Minnie M. Sweets Summers, *Deans of Girls in High Schools of Oklahoma*. Unpublished study, 1929.

[g] Opal R. Switzer, *Deans of Girls in Junior and Senior High Schools of the United States*. Unpublished study, 1928.

one hundred and fifty or more pupils reported that they have deans of girls. In two states almost half the schools reported having deans. In earlier studies, the per cent of schools reporting deans ranges from 50 to 67. This apparently higher percentage in previous studies is probably due (*a*) to the inclusion of larger schools which, as might be expected, employ deans more frequently than the smaller institutions; and (*b*) to the smaller percentage of replies received.

The proportion of high schools having deans of girls is much lower than the proportion of liberal arts colleges, universities, and teachers colleges and normal schools having deans of women. More than three-fourths of the higher institutions of learning have this officer.[1]

TITLE

The title which is most frequently used, which is preferred by deans, and which is sanctioned by the National Association of Deans of Women is that of "Dean of Girls." Three-fourths of the hundred deans in this study hold this title, and all but six find it satisfactory. The ten different titles reported, with the frequency of their occurrence, are as follows:

Title	Frequency
Dean of Girls	75
Adviser of Girls	12
Assistant Principal	3
Director of Extra-Curricular Activities	2
Administrative Assistant	2
Vice-principal	1
Guidance Counselor	1
Student Adviser	1
Counselor of Girls	1

Half of the women called "Advisers of Girls" prefer some other title. The term "Adviser" connotes to some pupils an officiousness which they resent. There is also, in the use of this title, a possible confusion with grade advisers. Certainly it inadequately describes the person who is not primarily interested in giving advice, but rather in providing a physical, social, and academic environment in which each pupil can develop to her maximum capacity.

[1] Colleges and universities, 93.3 per cent. (Jones, *op. cit.*, p. 12). Normal schools and teachers colleges, 77.0 per cent. (Sturtevant and Strang, *op. cit.*, p. 11.)

The titles of "Assistant Principal," "Vice-Principal," and "Administrative Assistant" often carry an increase in salary and the consequent prestige makes these titles acceptable to those who hold them. In some cases they imply a preponderance of administrative duties. In other cases the usual routine work of the vice-principal is delegated to a second assistant principal or other member of the staff, thus leaving the dean free to devote her time to the personal and social aspects of her work. In order to keep the professional rank implied by these titles and at the same time prevent the administrative aspects of the position from being over-emphasized, some women prefer to combine the titles and be called, for example, "Administrative Assistant and Dean of Girls."

Such a combination of titles would be unnecessary if the dean's function were clearly defined. The position of dean of girls would then be recognized in the educational world as at least equivalent in rank to that of assistant principal,[2] but carrying major social and personal as well as administrative responsibilities.

Rank Equivalent to That of Dean of Girls

One way in which the office of dean of girls may be defined is in terms of other positions in the school. Is the rank of the dean equivalent to that of assistant principal, head of department, or teacher?

Approximately three-fourths of the hundred selected deans hold the rank of assistant principal. In the smallest and the largest group of schools approximately two of every three deans are ranked as assistant principal. The largest proportion of deans having this rank is found in Group III (schools enrolling an average of 1,368 pupils).

Almost one-fifth of these deans serve as head of department. This rank is found more frequently in the larger than in the smaller schools.

The number of deans designated merely as teacher is negligible except in the smallest schools. Table V shows in detail the number

[2] Resolution of a joint committee of deans, school superintendents and principals on "Selection and Qualifications of Deans of Girls, meeting in Cleveland, February, 1929": "The term Dean of Girls should denote that person who is officially appointed in a given school to coördinate the interests and promote the general welfare of the girls, with special reference to the development of character and personality—both as individuals and as members of society. The dean's position should carry with it rank, authority, and salary at least equal to those of a vice-principal."

and percentage of deans holding ranks equivalent to those of assistant principal, head of department, or teacher. New York does not differ markedly from the rest of the country in this respect.

These facts are useful in understanding the dean's official position in secondary schools. In the majority of cases she is in an authoritative position ranking next to the principal. Such a position seems logical for the person who must supervise various

TABLE V

RANK IN SCHOOL EQUIVALENT TO THAT OF DEAN OF GIRLS

(100 Selected Deans)

RANK IN SCHOOL	GROUP I 321*		GROUP II 737		GROUP III 1368		GROUP IV 2751		TOTAL (ALL GROUPS)		NEW YORK STATE	
	Number	Per Cent	Number	Per Cent	Number	Per Cent	Number	Per Cent	Number	Per Cent	Number	Per Cent
Assistant principal	8	67	22	75	26	84	18	64	74	74	27	69
Head of department ...	0	0	5	17	4	13	9	32	18	18	10	25
Teacher	4	33	1	4	1	3	0	0	6	6	1	3
Others	0	0	0	0	0	0	0	0	0	0	1	3
Not stated	....	....	1	4	0	0	1	4	2	2	....	....
Number of cases	12		29		31		28		100		39	

* Mean total enrollment.

phases of the school life for all the girls in the school, and, in many cases, for the boys also where the social program involves both. To perform the duties of her office effectively requires advanced training and experience which should be recognized by promotion in rank and by the monetary rewards which accompany promotion.

METHOD OF APPOINTMENT OF DEAN OF GIRLS

A question of much concern to women desiring to become deans, and to principals contemplating appointing deans in their schools, is: Should deans be promoted from the faculty or should they be called to the position because of special training and aptitude for the work, regardless of previous experience in the particular school, and in spite of the desire of teachers for promotion?

Three-fourths of the deans in this study were selected from the faculty. This general tendency to promote teachers in the school to the position of dean is especially characteristic of the largest and smallest schools. Twenty-four deans in the twenty-eight schools enrolling more than a thousand girls were selected from the faculty. The following situation is probably typical of many others. In a school having almost three thousand pupils the woman chosen to be dean had been a teacher in the school for twelve years, and had, during some of these years, served voluntarily as club leader and grade adviser. She was at the time of her appointment head of the history department. After a term's leave of absence she returned to the school and found that she had been made "Administrative Assistant and Dean of Girls." She had been so popular with the other teachers of the school that apparently there was none of the jealousy which too frequently handicaps a dean promoted to the position from the faculty.

There are both advantages and disadvantages to this plan of promoting teachers within the school to the position of dean. The most obvious advantage is the intimate knowledge of pupils, teachers, community, and school customs and policies which the dean who has previously taught in the school has acquired. The chief disadvantages are the lack of specific training and experience in the dean's work, frequently found among teachers promoted to the position, and, in some cases, the handicap of being a "prophet without honor" in her own country. To overcome these disadvantages several progressive principals have chosen from their faculty a teacher who has shown special interest in and aptitude for work with individuals, and have given her a year's leave of absence in which to prepare for the work. In this way, by adding professional training to native ability, the principal may secure a person preëminently fitted for the position.

Some progressive superintendents, on the other hand, prefer to appoint as dean in their schools a person from outside the system who has had special training for the work. The advantages of this method are the new points of view which a person familiar with other schools brings and the prestige which her additional special training carries.

Another question regarding the appointing of deans which is of interest to people wishing to enter the vocation is: Is the salary usually increased to parallel the new responsibilities?

Of the 71 deans who replied to this question, 63 answered in the affirmative. Of these, 57 stated the amount of increase. The smallest increment was $50 per annum; the largest, $1,200; the average $318. The amounts increased with the size of schools. Table VI gives the facts concerning these aspects of the selection and appointment of deans for each group of schools.

TABLE VI

SELECTION AND APPOINTMENT OF DEANS OF GIRLS

(*100 Selected Deans*)

	GROUP I	GROUP II	GROUP III	GROUP IV	TOTAL (ALL GROUPS)
Dean selected from the faculty					
Yes	9	22	19	24	74
No	3	7	12	4	26
No. reporting	12	29	31	28	100
Salary increased on appointment					
Yes	9	17	17	20	63
No	0	5	2	1	8
No. reporting	9	22	19	21	71
Mean amount of salary increase	$228.57	$256.33	$356.25	$368.42	$318.33
No. specifying the increase	7	15	16	19	57

This table is read as follows: In the 12 schools in Group I, 9 deans were selected from the faculty; 3 were not. In these 9 cases the salary was increased on appointment. The average increase of salary in the case of the 7 deans who specified the exact amount of increase was $228.57, etc.

In general, it seems to be customary to increase the salary of teachers who are promoted to the new responsibilities of dean. This increase in salary is usually from $200 to $400. In certain large city schools the promotion from teacher to administrative assistant is accompanied by an increase in salary of more than a thousand dollars. Needless to say, this is exceptional rather than typical practice.

CHAPTER III

EXPERIENCE AND TRAINING OF DEANS OF GIRLS

There are many elements which enter into the making of a dean. Among other factors are her experience and education. Principals engaged in selecting a dean, and women preparing for the position, would be glad to know the experience and training which successful deans of girls have had. In other words, they would like to know the vocational path by which deans in service have reached their present positions. The vocational history blank on page four of the questionnaire (see Appendix B) was carefully filled out by ninety-eight deans and furnishes a wealth of interesting information concerning the devious routes to the position of dean of girls.

VARIETIES OF ACADEMIC, ADMINISTRATIVE, AND SOCIAL EXPERIENCE OF DEANS

Teaching Experience. Although the vocational history of each of the hundred deans is unique, there are certain features common to all. As might be expected, the position of dean is usually approachable via teaching. All but three deans have had some teaching experience, either in high school or in elementary school. Of these three, one had been a high school secretary for eight years, another a principal for seventeen years, and the third a successful Y. W. C. A. Girls' Work Secretary for ten years. The number of years of total teaching experience ranges from 0 to 27; the mean is 10.5 years. The range of teaching experience in elementary school is from 0 to 14 years; the mean is 1.4. Only thirty-five of these deans have taught in elementary school. All but seven have taught in high school from 0 to 27 years, the average being 8.9 years. With such a backgound of experience in elementary and high schools, deans should have acquired considerable insight into child psychology and an understanding of academic problems and policies of the secondary school.

Experience as Administrative Officers. Since one phase of the dean's work is administrative, previous executive experience should be helpful to her. Eighteen of this group have had experience as principal either in elementary or high school, previous to appointment in their present position. Fifteen have been heads of departments.

Experience in Advisory Work. Most significant is the incidental advisory work of this group. In their teaching positions, they were serving at the same time as club leaders, grade advisers, camp and playground directors, and other types of counselors. Experience of this kind is valuable in at least four ways: first, in testing the teacher's aptitude and ability to do advisory work; second, in giving her a first-hand basis of experience in the kind of work which she will later supervise; third, in extending her knowledge of girls through intimate association with them in a variety of situations; and fourth, in demonstrating to the principal and other members of the staff her special fitness for the position of dean.

Other Experiences of Value. Travel in the United States and in Europe, marriage, the rearing of children, secretarial work, newspaper experience, welfare work, and many other kinds of experience can be used advantageously in the dean's work. Such experience should be considered an asset to any candidate applying for the position.

This brief summary does not show the extraordinary diversity of experience which some individuals have had. The vocational history of two deans will illustrate the variety of work and study in which a number of this group have engaged.

Case I. After graduating from college, this dean studied music and German at home. For three years she taught the "three R's" in elementary school. This teaching experience was followed by a year of study abroad in two German universities. On her return to the United States she taught German and history for two years in a private school, and was principal of the school for two years. Her time during the next four years was occupied with work for a foreign travel bureau of which she was vice-president. After another year of study in college, she accepted a high school position in which she taught German and French for nine years, and also served as head of the department and adviser to girls during part of this period. In the summers she studied abroad and conducted a group of college girls in France. During 1926-1927 she became head of the modern language department and adviser of girls in another high school. The following year she returned to the university for more graduate study and majored in advisory work.

Case II. After one year of college and one year of study at the Chicago Froebel Association—this dean accepted a business position in order to earn money to continue her education. The following year she received her diploma in physical education from a state normal school. While a student at Chicago she did social work at Hull House, and while attending the normal school engaged in voluntary club work. Her first teaching experience was as supervisor of physical education in high school. She held this position for five years and served as club leader, faculty adviser, and supervisor of athletics at the Y. W. C. A. in addition to her official duties. She then married and spent four years at home. College again gained her attention for three years. At the end of this time she received a B. S. degree and returned to teaching in high school for eight years. One summer she spent in study at a school of oratory, and two others in graduate work in a teachers college. After her first summer session she accepted a position as dean of girls. In addition to all these experiences she has "directed playground and pageantry work for seventeen summers at independent Chautauquas over the country and has been in every state in the Union."

These two cases are illustrative rather than typical of the variety of educational, vocational, and avocational experience which some of these deans have had. The first case illustrates also the valuable cultural background which many of these deans possess.

Vocational Routes. The simplest vocational path to the dean's position in high school is by way of high school teaching. Thirty-seven deans went to college immediately after having been graduated from high school, and then taught in high school until they were officially appointed to supervise various aspects of the school life of all the girls. Those years of high school teaching, however, were, in three-fourths of the cases, interspersed with periods of graduate study (especially in summer sessions), travel, home life, and incidental advisory work.

Fifteen other deans have had both elementary and high school experience. The essential features of the vocational pattern of this group are:

> College or normal school education
> Teaching in elementary school
> Advanced study
> Teaching in high school
> Appointment as dean

Eighteen deans have attained their positions through administrative, as well as teaching, avenues. Their vocational history is as follows:

> College education
> Teaching either in elementary or high school
> Serving as principal or assistant principal
> Appointment as dean

Half of this group engages in graduate study, especially in summer sessions. They also mention valuable non-professional experience.

Intermediate in administrative functions between the teacher and the assistant principal is the head of department or supervisor. Nine deans reported holding one of these positions previous to, or parallel with, their work as deans.

Six deans have run almost the whole gamut of elementary and high school positions before finding their way to the dean's office. They have taught in elementary school and high school, have been head of a department, and assistant principal or principal. Two were in business, one was director of an evening school, one taught in college during summer sessions, and another, in addition to her experience as elementary teacher, high school teacher, head of department, and high school principal, brought up seven children one of whom has acquired the degree of Doctor of Philosophy; two of the degree of Master of Arts; and a fourth the degree of Doctor of Medicine.

The remaining vocational histories defied classification. In one case the efficient woman who had served as school secretary for eight years was appointed dean. Although she has had no teaching experience, she has acquired 30 points of graduate study in education beyond the Master's degree. Another dean held the position of assistant dean and assistant professor in a junior college before she entered the high school field. One dean was a private tutor before she became a public school teacher. The professional experience of four deans was chiefly in social and Y. W. C. A. work. One of these deans did outstanding work for ten years as a Y. W. C. A. Girls' Work Secretary. She next took a professional course for advisers of women, and accepted a position as acting dean in a college during summer session. Following this experience she was made dean of girls in a large high school during the academic year. Very seldom does graduate work follow directly after graduation from college. These deans usually continue their study after having had some teaching experience.

Judging from the vocational histories of these deans, an ideal route to the dean's position seems to be:

Graduation from college
Teaching in high school
Administrative experience as principal, assistant principal or head of department
Incidental advisory work and travel
Graduate study in the dean's field

That this vocational route is not an impractical one is indicated by the fact that many of its features are common to the majority of this group of selected deans.

EDUCATIONAL HISTORY

Preparation for the vocation of dean of girls includes academic training as well as experience. Scholastic achievement is represented in a general way by the degrees held.

Academic Degrees. Table VII shows the degrees held by one hundred deans. Since this is a selected group, the percentage of women holding higher degrees may be larger than the percentage for all deans of girls in the United States. New York State, for example, is slightly inferior to the hundred deans in this respect. It will be seen from the table that 95 per cent have acquired at least a Bachelor's degree and 38 per cent, a Master's degree. None of this group have secured a doctorate. There are, however, as indicated by other studies, a few high school deans in this country

TABLE VII

DEGREES HELD BY DEANS OF GIRLS

(100 Selected Deans)

DEGREE	GROUP I		GROUP II		GROUP III		GROUP IV		TOTAL (ALL GROUPS)	
	Number	Per Cent	Number	Per Cent	Number	Per Cent	Number	Per Cent	Number	Per Cent
No degree	0	.....	1	3	0	.....	1	3	2	2
Bachelor's degree										
B.A.	8	67	18	62	27	87	21	75	74	74
B.S.	3	25	6	21	3	10	3	11	15	15
Others	0	.....	2	7	1	3	3	11	6	6
Total, having at least a bachelor's degree	11	92	26	90	31	100	27	96	95	95
Master's degree	2	17	11	38	12	39	13	46	38	38
Number reporting	12	100	29	100	31	100	28	100	100	100

Table VII is read as follows: Of the 12 deans in Group I, none are without a degree of some kind; 8, or 67 per cent, hold a Bachelor of Arts degree; 3, or 25 per cent, hold a Bachelor of Science degree. No other kinds of Bachelor's degrees were mentioned; 11, or 92 per cent, hold at least the Bachelor's degree; and 2, or 17 per cent, the Master's degree, etc.

who have obtained the Doctor's degree. In liberal arts colleges and universities [1] the percentage of deans having the Bachelor's degree is 90.5, and of those having the Master's degree, 57.4. In teachers colleges and normal schools,[2] the percentages are 86.3 and 41.1, respectively. It will be noted that more high school deans of girls have the Bachelor's degree than deans in higher institutions, but the deans in high schools have fewer Master's degrees to their credit.

In addition to obtaining these degrees, many deans have had academic training which has not yet culminated in a degree.

Professional Courses. In addition to the general training indicated by degrees and other college courses, eighty-one of these one hundred deans have taken a professional course in advisory

[1] Jones, J. L., *op. cit.*, p. 18.
[2] Sturtevant, Sarah M. and Strang, Ruth, *op. cit.*, p. 18.

work. In Groups II and III more than 90 per cent of the deans have taken a professional course. The percentages in the smallest and in the largest schools are lower. These eighty-one deans have taken courses for advisers given at Teachers College, Columbia University, the Universities of California, Chicago, Washington, Minnesota, Wisconsin, and Missouri, and Harvard University, Boston University, Leland Stanford University, and the State College of Oregon.

It must be remembered that this is a selected group and probably is in advance of the average dean in this respect. Professional training is in itself an evidence of professional interest. Accordingly, those who have had professional training are likely to constitute a large proportion of this group.

A professional course, as everyone knows, does not make a successful dean; but added to other desirable personal characteristics and experience, it should enable the dean to see her position "steadily and whole," and should give her knowledge of principles and procedures which she could not secure so easily and systematically in any other way. A professional course ought to be especially valuable to teachers with advisory experience who are soon to be appointed to the dean's position, and to deans in service who wish to keep in touch with new developments in their field.

SUMMARY

The background of this group of deans is in general a varied one. It includes teaching in elementary and high schools, administrative work as head of department or principal, incidental advisory work, and other social and cultural contacts. The noticeable feature of this characteristic experience is that it is diverse rather than narrowly specialized—and would tend to give insight into life rather than technical knowledge of some branch of subject matter.

To the cultural background, practical experience, and four years of graduate study, 81 per cent of these deans have added professional training in the field of advisement of women and girls.

These vocational histories indicate that the work of the dean of girls, as of the dean of women in colleges and teacher training institutions, is of an educational and professional nature, but at the same time social and diverse in its aspects; that the standards which demand a high type of education, experience, and professional training are not impractical and theoretical, but rather descriptive of the preparation and training of outstanding deans in this country.

CHAPTER IV

SALARIES OF DEANS OF GIRLS

Deans might with justice expect a salary commensurate with the extensive and expensive preparation described in the previous chapter. Women considering advisory work as a possible vocation wish to know the salary which they may expect to receive after the completion of a certain period of preparation. Principals, also, are interested in having their deans receive a just recompense.

SALARIES RECEIVED

Individual Differences in Salary. The variations in rank, title, preparation, and training previously noted suggest comparable variations in salary. This expectation is fulfilled. Table VIII gives a condensed distribution of the salaries of these hundred deans, and makes possible a comparison of the salaries of deans with those of high school principals and teachers. The wide range and the large standard deviations indicate the lack of standardization, in the dean's position, in this aspect. Even within a group of a given size, the salaries vary from approximately one thousand to four thousand dollars.

Average Salary.[1] The medium salary of the hundred deans in this study is $2,588. There is an increase in the mean salary of approximately $200 to $300 from group to group, as the schools become larger. Half of the hundred deans receive between $2,218 and $3,200 annually; one-fourth receive less than $2,218; and one-fourth, more than $3,200. It will be seen from Table VIII that the salaries of deans, as might be expected in view of their rank in the school, is, generally speaking, lower than the principals' and higher than that of high school teachers.*

The median salary of these high school deans is $178.60 less than the median for deans in colleges and universities,[2] and

---

[1] Both the mean and the median were computed because the extreme cases in some of the distributions make the mean a little less reliable than it usually is.

[2] Jones, J. L., *op. cit.*, p. 52.

TABLE VIII

Annual Salaries of Deans of Girls in High School

(100 Selected Deans)

	Group I	Group II	Group III	Group IV	Total (All Groups)	High School Princi- pals*	High School Teach- ers*
							Below
Lowest	$1,480.00	$1,560.00	$1,600.00	$1,800.00	$1,480.00	$1,350.00	$1,000.00
Q₁	1,700.00	2,084.00	2,350.00	2,600.00	2,218.18		
Median	2,200.00	2,472.00	2,825.00	3,080.00	2,588.00	4,193.00	2,120.00
Q₃	2,320.00	2,950.00	3,362.50	3,500.00	3,200.00		
Highest	2,600.00	3,300.00	4,800.00	5,688.00	5,688.00	6,000.00 and over	4,000.00 and over
Mean	2,008.67	2,441.10	2,738.32	3,224.86	2,720.80		
S.D.	360.00	500.00	636.00	524.00	820.00		
Number of cases	12	29	31	28	100		

This table is read as follows: In the 12 schools in Group I (schools enrolling from 250 to 500 pupils), the lowest salary is $1,480. One-fourth of this group receive a salary of less than $1,700, one-half receive less than $2,200, and three-fourths receive less than $2,320. The highest salary is $2,600. The average salary of this group is $2,008.67, and the standard deviation, 360, etc.

* *Salary Scales in City School Systems, 1928–29,* Research Bulletin of the National Education Association, Washington, D. C. High schools in cities 30,000–100,000. Principals, p. 125, Teachers, p. 120, 123.

$466.00 less than the median for deans in teacher training institutions.[3] Since the deans in higher institutions frequently serve in summer session, the salary of high school deans in terms of service actually rendered compares favorably with that of deans in colleges and normal schools.

Factors Influencing the Salary of High School Deans of Girls

Location of School. The salary of deans varies from state to state. An investigation of the dean's position in New York State shows that the median salary of deans in this state is $762 higher than that of the hundred selected deans. This high average salary is due to thirteen administrative assistants who do dean's work to such an extent as to be so classed and who receive an annual salary of $5,688. Figures compiled by the National Education

[3] Sturtevant and Strang, *op. cit.,* p. 26.

Association [4] show a large variation in the median salary of deans in cities having a population of more than 100,000. For example, the median salary of deans in Texas is $2,300, while in Illinois it is $4,104. This variation in salary in different states may be due either to a difference in the general salary schedule of the states or to a difference in the definition of the dean's position. In states in which the dean usually holds a rank equivalent to that of assistant principal, her salary is higher than in states in which she is on the same level as teachers or department heads. The salary of deans also varies with the size of city in which the school is located. This fact is most clearly shown by the figures of the National Education Association.[5] The median salary of all deans reporting in cities of from 30,000 to 100,000 population is $2,555; while the median salary in cities over 100,000 is $3,000. We should accordingly expect the salary of deans in cities like New York, Newark, and Chicago to be proportionately large, as is the case.

Size of School. Size of school is usually associated with size of city, and consequently we should expect the salaries of deans in schools of Group I to be smaller than those of schools in Group IV. That such is the case may be readily seen in Table VIII. The difference in salary between the means of Group I and Group IV is $1,216 ± $98. A difference of more than four times the probable error is generally considered to be a significant one. This difference is more than twelve times the probable error. We can assume, therefore, that size of school is one factor in the amount of salary which the dean receives.

Academic Training of Deans. It would be encouraging to educators, if salary were proportional to training. This is not always the case, however. The difference between the mean salary of deans holding the Master's degree and the mean salary of those having only the Bachelor's degree is $329 ± $106, in favor of the Master's degree. No significance can be attached to this difference since it is little more than three times the probable error. In fact, in Group II the mean salary of deans holding the

[4] *Salary Scale in City School Systems, 1928-1929,* Research Bulletin of the National Education Association, Vol. VII, No. 3, p. 115, May, 1929. 1201 Sixteenth Street, Northwest, Washington, D. C.

[5] *Op. cit.,* pp. 115, 120.

Bachelor's degree is $31 more than that of deans who have acquired the Master's degree also. It must not be concluded, however, that graduate study has no influence on salary, but rather that there are other more potent factors which determine the amount of money which a given dean receives.

Rank. The difference between the mean salary of deans having the rank of assistant principal and those holding the rank of department head is $304.34 ± $106.59. As in the case of academic training, this difference is insignificant. The difference between the salary of the seventy-four deans having the rank of assistant principal and the six deans having the rank of teacher is $438.46. The numbers in this case, however, are too small to warrant any general conclusion.

Hours of Teaching. The mean salary of the 36 deans who do no teaching is $3,082.31; of the 21 deans teaching from 5 to 10 hours, $2,928.95; of the 16 deans having a teaching load of from 10 to 15 hours, $2,400.63; of the 20 deans teaching 15 to 20 hours, $2,232.70; and of the 7 deans teaching from 20 to 25 hours, $2,050. Although there is practically no difference in salary between deans who teach less than one period a day and those who teach one to two periods, the difference between the other groups is larger. Between those who teach zero hours and 10-15 hours

TABLE IX

Salaries of Deans According to Age

(*100 Selected Deans*)

Age	Number of Cases	Mean Salary
25–29	6	$1,328.33
30–34	17	2,597.59
35–39	19	2,526.05
40–44	25	2,697.92
45–49	16	2,779.06
50–54	7	3,675.43
55–59	3	3,466.67
60–64	1	1,500.00
Total reporting and mean salary	94	2,720.80

the difference in salary is $681.68 ± $150.92; between those who teach zero and 15-20 hours the difference in salary is $849.61 ± 128.20. These differences are sufficiently large to indicate a significant negative relationship between salary and hours of teaching. The deans who have the heaviest teaching load are frequently the ones receiving the lowest salaries. Teaching load, however, may not be significant in itself but may be merely one factor which is associated with others such as age of the incumbent, size of school, and indefinite professional status of the dean, which all exert an influence on salary.

Age. Do older deans receive higher salaries than younger women? Table IX shows a general tendency for the mean salary of deans to increase up to fifty years of age.

No Single Factor. The salaries of deans seem to be related to a number of factors, a combination of which would probably result in the highest salary. For example, a dean having the rank of assistant principal in a large school in a city system, holding the Master's degree, having a long record of service in the school, and carrying a small teaching load is probably receiving a fairly large salary.

This is only one of a number of combination of factors which may result in a large salary. It is, however, not fair to say that these objective and impersonal factors are the causes of higher salaries, but they usually indicate personal qualities which bear a relation to salary. For example, a winning personality may compensate for a small amount of academic training, and special ability, for a short term of service. The woman who has all of these assets can be most confident of remuneration equal to her experience, training, and native capacity. Table X shows the relation of some of these factors to salary.

SUMMARY

The range of annual salary for these hundred deans is $1,480-$5,688. Half of this group receive less than $2,588 per year and half receive more than this amount. If the salary of these deans is representative of the salary of high school deans in the United States, there is a one to one chance that any particular dean will receive between $2,218 and $3,200. If she be appointed in a large

TABLE X

SALARIES OF DEANS COMPARED WITH HOURS OF TEACHING, LENGTH OF
SERVICE AND RANK

(100 Selected Deans)

	GROUP I	GROUP II	GROUP III	GROUP IV	TOTAL (ALL GROUPS)
Mean salary	$2,008.67	$2,441.10	$2,738.32	$3,224.86	$2,720.80
Mean number of hours of teaching	16.7	9.5	5.0	3.9	7.4
Mean length of service in the school	7.0	8.0	7.0	13.4*	9.1
Mean length of service as dean	3.3	4.6	4.4	7.1	5.1
Per cent ranked as assistant- or vice-principal	69	77	84	67	76
Per cent ranked as head of department	0	19	13	33	18
Per cent ranked as teacher	31	4	3	0	6
Number of cases	12	29	31	28	100

This table is read as follows: The mean salary of deans in Group I—
schools enrolling 250 to 499 pupils—is $2,008.67. The mean number of hours
of teaching for this group is 16.7; the mean length of service in the school,
7 hours; and the mean length of service as dean, 3.3 hours. Sixty-nine per
cent of this group hold the rank of assistant principal; none, the rank of
head of department; and 31 per cent the rank of teacher only, etc.

* This mean is influenced by six deans who had periods of service of twenty years
or more.

city system and given the rank of assistant principal, her salary
may exceed $5,000. As far as salary is concerned, it apparently
makes little difference which educational level—high school, normal school, teachers college, liberal arts college, or university—is
selected as a person's vocational field.

CHAPTER V

DUTIES OF DEANS OF GIRLS

The summary of the answers to the questions [1] concerning the duties of deans of girls may be of interest to principals, deans, and teachers. Principals and deans in service are interested in knowing the duties which deans in other schools perform. Women preparing for advisory positions need to know the duties which are frequently required of deans. High school teachers, nurses, and other school officers should see more clearly their relationship to the dean, and their opportunities for coöperation with her.

It is obvious that the distinction between those duties performed by the dean personally, and those for which her office is responsible should be kept clearly in mind. As an administrator she may, like the principal, plan, delegate, and supervise many phases of work which she could not possibly personally handle. In large schools the tendency is evidently in the direction of working through others. On the other hand, there are duties which frequently rest solely with the dean as far as the *official* handling of them is concerned. An attempt was made to get at this difference by asking whether she performed a given duty "alone?" The latter case might be the result of coöperation directed by the dean as an administrator, or of delegation by the principal of similar duties to various people over whom the dean has no supervision. In trying to get at so intangible a factor as coöperation, it is obvious that the most that can be hoped is to discover the most common avenues and most common types of coöperation which the dean of girls may expect.

This chapter will attempt to answer the following questions:

1. Which specific duties are performed by the majority of these hundred deans, either alone or in coöperation with others?

2. Which duties do they think deans *should* perform?

3. To what extent are these deans solely responsible for specific

[1] See pp. 5-12 of the questionnaire, Appendix B.

duties? To what extent do they coöperate with others? Which members of the school staff frequently assist the dean?

4. Which duties take the largest amount of the dean's time?

5. Is night work necessary? If so, what kinds?

6. Does the dean hold regular office hours? Which kinds of work occupy the major part of her office hours?

Duties Performed by the Majority of the Deans Studied

Arranged in order of frequency, the following duties are performed by at least three-fourths of the hundred deans in this study.[2] The corresponding frequency for the New York State deans is also included.

Duty	One Hundred Selected Deans. Frequency	Thirty-nine Deans in New York State. Frequency
1. Extend influence with girls through informal contact	96	32
2. Interview girls who come voluntarily to the dean with social problems	94	35
3. Confer with principals and teachers concerning the academic work of girls	94	34
4. Attend faculty meetings	94	36
5. Read and answer correspondence	94	28
6. Attend conferences of professional people	94	36
7. Interview parents	93	38
8. Interview girls who come voluntarily with home difficulties	92	36
9. Extend influence with faculty through informal contact	90	29
10. Read recent articles on personnel work	90	33
11. Attend assembly periods	89	31
12. Interview girls who come voluntarily with financial difficulties	88	33
13. Assist committees of girls in planning social events	88	26
14. Interview girls referred for failure in academic work	87	31
15. Attend meetings of many extra-curriculum activities	87	28
16. Discover cases of unsocial girls	85	31
17. Assist principal and faculty in policy making ..	85	33
18. Take a professional course for deans	85	27

[2] More details concerning the duties performed in the school, those performed by the dean, those performed by some one else, and those which deans think they should perform, may be found in Appendix C.

Duty	One Hundred Selected Deans. Frequency	Thirty-nine Deans in New York State. Frequency
19. Address or secure speakers to address groups of girls	84	22
20. Interview girls who come voluntarily with employment problems	82	30
21. Discover cases of over-social girls	81	32
22. Interview girls who come voluntarily with health problems	80	28
23. Officially entertain school visitors	80	24
24. Confer with officers and committees of girls' organizations	79	27
25. Confer with sponsors of girls' organizations	79	23
26. Interview girls referred for health problems	78	29
27. Discover cases of girls below par in health	77	30
28. Prepare reports from time to time	77	26
29. Initiate new extra-curriculum activities	76	24
30. Interview girls who come with personal problems of all kinds	76	28
31. Direct social life and extra-curriculum activities of girls	75	21
32. Check and change pupils' programs during the year	75	23
33. Handle emergency case of illness	75	22

There may be noted in this list of duties a constructive emphasis upon informal contact with pupils, parents, and teachers; interviews with girls who come voluntarily with personal problems; direction of group activities by means of conferences with officers and sponsors of clubs, and with committees of students; professional reading and conferences; interviews and meetings with principal and teachers regarding school policies and the academic work of girls. A dean and principal studying this list of duties would find it difficult to omit any of them from a program of personnel work in the school. Whether the dean herself performs a given duty depends upon a number of factors: the size of the school, the number and training of the people on her staff, the interest and ability of the teachers, and the time at their disposal for advisory work; the special officers employed by the school such as vocational guidance expert, health education director, and attendance secretary; the needs of the pupils; the deans' own experience and training; and the principal's vision of the dean's work.

Using as a check list the duties performed by these hundred deans, a dean in a particular situation may decide whether or not a given duty should be performed in the school, who are the best persons in the school to perform it, and how their coöperation may be gained and assistance given them in the performance of the duty.

Duties Which Deans Think They Should Perform

Although all the deans did not answer this question either because they had no decided opinion on the subject or because they lacked time, nevertheless the responses indicate a certain amount of agreement concerning the dean's functions.

From the table in Appendix C it will be noted that in the majority of cases these deans are doing the work they believe properly belongs to their office. As might be expected, they wish to keep in touch with new developments in their field by reading, visiting other schools, and attending conferences. They agree, of course, that the dean should interview girls who come voluntarily with their personal problems. They think deans should discover cases of maladjustment more frequently than they do at present. Apparently, they appreciate the importance of recognizing defects of health and personality in the early stages in which remedial measures are most effective.

Eighty of these women recognize the relation of the dean to the social aspects of the school environment. If a normal social life for boys and girls is provided, many behavior problems that would otherwise develop will never arise. The majority of these deans agree that supervision of pupils' conduct in the cafeteria and in other parts of the school building, initiating new activities as they are needed, assisting committees in planning social events, attending meetings of extra-curriculum activities, and assisting in chaperoning school affairs, are social functions which the dean should perform in conjunction with other members of the institution.

Orientation of freshmen is also considered one of the dean's functions, although it is not very systematically performed at present.

Sixty-eight deans think that they should coöperate with the vocational director, head of the commercial department, or whoever is in charge of the vocational guidance and placement work.

Information in the dean's office frequently advantageously supplements the data which these other workers have gathered, since conferences on personal problems sometimes reveal vocational and economic difficulties.

This group of deans feel a keen responsibility for the health of girls, and believe that they can contribute to an adequate health program (1) by supervising the health equipment and sanitary conditions of the building; (2) by emphasizing the health objectives in education; (3) by discovering and following up cases of girls below par in health; (4) by interviewing girls referred to them because of health problems; and (5) by handling emergency cases of illness. Their point of view in regard to all of these duties seems to be: This important work must be done in the school; if it is being done satisfactorily by a special officer and committees, the dean has little further responsibility except to coöperate with this officer whenever she can be of assistance. If the health program is inadequate, the dean herself must temporarily perform some of the duties connected with care for the health of girls until other people who are more adequately prepared are secured to do the work.

There is less agreement in regard to the dean's part in the academic life of the school. Most deans agree that they should interview girls who come to them voluntarily with study problems. A smaller number wish to interview girls referred for failure in academic work. Sixty-six recognize the importance of discovering the intellectually superior and inferior pupils. In general, apparently, this group believes that the primary responsibility for the scholastic achievement of pupils rests upon the teacher rather than upon the dean.

It will be seen from the table in Appendix C that there are very few duties which many of these women think that the dean should perform alone. In fact, many state positively that the dean should *not* work single-handedly in the orienting of freshmen, in giving guidance in study and health problems, in interviewing all cases of absence and tardiness, in administering discipline, in discovering and following up cases of maladjustment, in giving vocational and educational guidance, in administering loans and scholarships, in handling emergency cases of illness, in directing social life and extra-curriculum activities, in supervising the sanitary and social conditions in the school, and in controlling the intellectual environment of the girls. In short, these deans recognize the interpenetration of their work through the whole school, and the necessity for the assistance of many persons. In actual performance of duties this coöperative nature of the dean's work necessitates the organization and supervision of a department of student life which shall correlate the various contributions of the faculty and give meaning to the whole process.

Extent of Coöperation of the Dean with Others

That this idea of coöperation is not a theoretical concept only, but also a practical working policy among deans is evident from the data gathered. There are no duties which all the deans in this group perform alone. The table in Appendix C shows the extent to which other people work with the dean. Giving guidance in study and health problems, supervising the sanitary and social aspects of the environment, making academic programs, personally chaperoning school affairs, administering discipline, interviewing girls who are absent or tardy, supervising financial aspects of girls' organizations, making available worthwhile books and magazines, personally supervising the student government organization, assisting in the placement of girls after graduation, supervising the health program, organizing social life among the faculty —all these duties are performed by the doctor, nurse, principal, special teachers, home-room teachers, faculty advisers, club sponsors, vocational guidance directors, health directors, or other members of the staff more frequently than they are performed by the dean.

There are, however, marked differences in the extent to which individual deans work with their associates. A few deans reported that they perform most of the duties alone; others coöperate with members of the faculty in every phase of their work. In a few cases a fine relationship with pupils and outside agencies was indicated.

Duties Requiring the Largest Amount of the Dean's Total Time

Data from Questionnaires. The data showing the quantitative aspect of the dean's work indicate two main divisions of her work—personal advisement of girls and supervision of group activities.

All but one of the hundred deans answered the question:

"Which three types of work take the largest amount of your time?" Table XI shows that eighty-one deans spend more time in the personal advisement of pupils than in any other way. The time spent in teaching, however, was not included in the answers to this question.

The supervision of group activities is the duty consuming the next largest amount of time. In schools of all sizes this supervision is done to the greatest extent through committee work with pupils.

Although many deans do not approve of spending a large amount of time in checking attendance and interviewing pupils concerning absence and tardiness, thirty-seven report this as one of the three duties occupying the largest amount of their time.

Table XI shows only seven cases in which routine office work consumes a major amount of the dean's time. Further discussion of this table is unnecessary, for the table itself may be studied by readers who are interested.

The types of duties to which these deans devote the largest amount of their office time are shown in Table XII. The same emphasis on personal advisement and supervision of group activities was found in this as in the answers to the previous questions. Conferences with teachers and principal and work with attendance were two other aspects of the dean's work occupying a large portion of their office time.

Data from Daily Schedules. More accurate quantitative information concerning the amount of time which deans of girls spend in various activities was obtained from the daily schedules kept for a period of two weeks by twenty-one high school deans.[3] The following section of one of the schedules illustrates the form used:

Monday
8:15 Supervision of bulletin board, appropriate books and magazines placed in the social room.
8:30 Conference with committee on spring carnival.
8:45 Conference with Bulletin Board Committee.
8:55 Conference with committee on Mother's Day program for general assembly.

[3] These schedules were tabulated, interpreted, and summarized by Miss Verna A. Carley and Mrs. Barbara A. L. Hewlett, graduate students in the department of Advisers of Women, Teachers College, Columbia University. The list of deans coöperating in this laborious task, to whom grateful acknowledgment is here made, is given in Appendix A.

TABLE XI

DUTIES, OTHER THAN TEACHING, CONSUMING THE LARGEST AMOUNT OF
THE DEAN'S TOTAL TIME AS REPORTED BY *(100 Selected Deans)*

	LARGEST AMOUNT OF TIME	NEXT LARGEST AMOUNT OF TIME	THIRD LARGEST AMOUNT OF TIME	TOTAL	
				Number	Per Cent
Personal advisement	81	12	1	94	95
Schedules and programs	0	4	4	8	8
Vocational guidance	0	1	1	2	2
Discipline	0	3	1	4	4
Scholarship	2	3	1	6	6
Group activities of pupils					
Committee work with pupils	2	26	12	40	40
Directing extra-curriculum activities	5	7	20	32	32
Supervision of student government	0	1	1	2	2
Conferences (general)	0	7	10	17	17
With principal and others concerning school policies and plans	1	6	4	10	10
With parents	0	1	4	5	5
Home visits	0	1	1	2	2
Administrative duties	1	3	3	7	7
Routine office work	0	3	4	7	7
Supervision of classroom work	0	0	1	1	1
Health supervision	0	1	3	4	4
Nursing	1	0	0	1	1
Emergency cases of illness	0	1	2	3	3
Attendance					
Follow-up of absence	0	0	1	1	1
Excuses	8	15	13	36	36
Informal personal contacts .	0	0	4	4	4
Number reporting, 99.					

This table is read: Personal advisement was the greatest time-consuming
duty for 81 deans; the second greatest for 12; the third greatest for 1.
Ninety-four, or 95 per cent, mentioned personal advisement as one of the
three greatest time-consuming duties.

9:10 Conference with student council president and chairman of committee on student conduct.

9:30 Advice ¹to girl who was ill.

9:32 Excused ill girl.

9:33 Spoke to home-room teacher concerning thrift work in her room.

9:40 Got material together concerning vocational work of Zonta women with girls of league.

TABLE XII

TYPE OF DUTIES CONSUMING THE LARGEST AMOUNT OF THE DEAN'S OFFICE TIME

(100 Selected Deans)

	GROUP I	GROUP II	GROUP III	GROUP IV	TOTAL (ALL GROUPS)	
	Number	Number	Number	Number	Number	Per Cent
Personal advisement						
Educational guidance	4	11	13	6	34	35
Vocational guidance	0	3	1	0	4	4
Personal guidance	9	25	29	26	89	92
Social adjustment (discipline)	3	7	0	6	16	16
Group activities of students	10	14	24	18	66	68
Conferences with						
Teachers	1	4	6	6	17	18
Advisers	0	0	1	0	1	1
Parents	1	3	4	3	11	11
Outside agencies	0	0	1	0	1	1
Administrative duties			1	4	5	5
Conference with principal	1	5	7	1	14	14
Records	0	2	2	1	5	5
Clerical work (office routine)	1	0	2	3	6	6
Attendance	2	12	8	3	25	26
Other duties	1	4	1	2	8	8
Number reporting	12	27	30	28	97	

This table is read as follows: Four of the 12 deans in Group I—schools enrolling 250-499 pupils—reported "educational guidance" as one of the three kinds of work that take the major part of their office time. In Group II, 11 deans mentioned this duty; in Group III, 13; in Group IV, 6. Altogether 34, or 35 per cent, of the 97 deans answering this question reported educational guidance as one of their three major office-hour occupations, etc.

The length of the professional day of these twenty-one deans varies from 6.42 to 12.8 hours. One dean spends more than twelve hours a day; three, approximately 10 hours; three, approximately 9 hours; six, 8 hours; seven, between 7 and 8 hours, and one, slightly less than 7 hours. The fourteen deans in schools enrolling more than one thousand pupils, work longer hours, on the average, than those in schools having an enrollment of less than one thousand pupils.

The number of different duties performed by the twenty-one individual deans ranges from 26 to 48. Eight duties are common to all. They are:

(1) Interviewing pupils concerning health problems.

(2) Interviewing pupils concerning absence and tardiness.

(3) Interviewing teachers, officers, and organizations concerning personal problems of pupils.

(4) Conferring with sponsors of clubs and social events.

(5) Conferring with principal or teachers concerning absence and the academic work of pupils.

(6) Studying, reading professional material, taking courses, and preparing lesson plans.

(7) Reading and answering correspondence.

(8) Miscellaneous office duties.

Significant differences in the amount of time spent in certain specific duties may be noted in Table XIII between the schools enrolling more than a thousand pupils and those enrolling less than a thousand. It will be seen that in both groups teaching occupies the largest average amount of the dean's time. In the larger schools attending meetings and social events as a guest or as a chaperon takes the second largest amount of the dean's time, and is a part of her work as supervisor of the social program. Four deans devote more than an hour a day to it; only one spent no time in this activity during the two weeks recorded. In the smaller schools, the deans spend, on the average, only half as much time in this way, probably because of fewer social activities.

Exclusive of teaching, miscellaneous office duties, including answering the telephone, keeping records, and writing reports occupy the largest amount of time of the deans in the smaller schools and the third largest amount of time in the schools enrolling more than a thousand pupils. Fourteen of the twenty-one deans in this

TABLE XIII

COMPARISON OF LARGE AND SMALL SCHOOLS AS TO THE TIME SPENT IN PERFORMING SPECIFIC DUTIES

(*Study of Schedules of 21 Deans*)

DUTY	LARGE SCHOOLS (Enrollment of 1000 or More. 14 Cases) Number of Minutes Per Day			SMALLER SCHOOLS (Enrollment of Less Than 1000. 7 Cases) Number of Minutes Per Day		
	Lowest	Mean	Highest	Lowest	Mean	Highest
Teaching	0	52	230	0	115	208
Directing social life by attending meetings and social events as guest or chaperon	0	37	102	0	19	29
Miscellaneous office duties	5	30	58	2	25	66
Personal development of the dean	3	29	96	0	20	54
Interviewing teachers, officers, and organizations concerning personal problems of pupils and educational policies	4	26	73	2	15	32
Interviewing pupils concerning absence and tardiness	3	19	47	1	24	49
Educational guidance, including advice concerning academic programs, choice of college, etc.	0	13	65	0	19	110
Conferring with principal and teachers concerning the academic work of pupils	2	17	52	0	17	43
Interviewing parents, including telephone calls with parents .	0	17	43	0	16	40

This table is read as follows: In the group of 14 large schools in this study of daily schedules, the smallest amount of time spent in teaching was 0; the largest, 230 minutes; and the average, 52 minutes per day. In the 7 smaller schools, the range was from 0 to 208, and the average, 115 minutes per day, etc.

TABLE XIV

PERCENTAGE OF TIME SPENT IN TYPES OF ACTIVITY BY DEANS IN SCHOOLS WITH AN ENROLLMENT OF 1000 OR MORE

(Study of Schedules, 14 Cases)

ACTIVITY	1	2	3	4	5	6	7	8	9	10	11	12	13	14	Aver.
I. Personal advisement	16.7	21.7	29	26	20.4	55.8	14.2	38.7	21	10.5	22.2	19.1	27.2	18.3	24.2
II. Group activities	20.1	8.8	2.5	39.5	36.1	11.5	29.9	22.8	17.1	25.5	22.2	50	5.4	44.3	24.4
III. Control of physical environment	3.4	1.8	9.5	1	7.9	1.1	6.9		.7	2.1	1.8	5.5	1.2	.2	2.8
IV. Control of intellectual environment	32.7	32.9	18.9	14.8	14.8	6.4	13.9	6.1	27.6	28.8	27	4.9	15.5	1	16.2
V. Personal development of Dean	7.2	12.4	7.1	7	3.6	4.2	8.5	.4	5.8	4.8	1.8	1.9	5.7	9.7	6
VI. Management of Dean's office	9	6.3	19.8	4	13.2	9.3	10.8	8.5	6.7	12.5	7.4	9.1	13.8	10.1	9.6
VII. Miscellaneous marginal duties	8.6	15.9	13.1	7.5	3.8	11.6	15.6	23.4	20.7	15.7	17.9	9.1	31.2	16.2	15.9

study spent more than 20 minutes a day in this duty; one spent 102 minutes. Whether or not the time spent in these office duties is time well spent depends upon the specific kind of work done. If the dean is doing mechanical work which can as well be delegated to clerks, the conclusion must be drawn that she has not yet successfully subjugated the routine office work to her more important constructive work with individuals. If, on the other hand, she is spending the time in making case studies, speaking with parents over the telephone, and writing reports on various phases of her work, the time spent in these ways is a necessary basis for her more direct advisory work.

The activity which ranks fourth in the amount of time spent by these deans contributes to the professional development of the dean herself.

Tables XIV and XV show the wide variation in the time given to different duties by deans in both groups of schools. Many striking individual differences in the average expenditure of time may be noted. For example, in the larger schools (Table XIV),

TABLE XV

PERCENTAGE OF TIME SPENT ON TYPES OF ACTIVITIES BY DEANS IN
SCHOOLS HAVING AN ENROLLMENT OF LESS THAN 1000

(*Study of Schedules, 7 Cases*)

ACTIVITY	1	2	3	4	5	6	7	Aver.
I. Personal advisement	28.4	29.5	29.2	7.6	36.3	7.0	12.7	22.0
II. Group activities	12.6	9.1	14.9	14.8	17.2	8.1	13.0	12.8
III. Control of physical environment	3.1	0.3	3.9	0.1	1.7	0.3	0.3	1.3
IV. Control of intellectual environment .	1.1	42.7	5.7	45.7	28.5	52.3	43.6	39.6
V. Personal development of dean	4.5	12.8	9.8	17.6		7.9	5.9	8.0
VI. Management of dean's office	22.0	2.6	4.4	7.4	7.4	5.9	13.7	9.2
VII. Miscellaneous marginal duties	17.9	2.6	6.1	8.8	8.6	18.2	10.8	10.5

This table is read as follows: In the personal advisement of students, one dean spent 16.7 per cent of her professional day during the two weeks in which she kept daily schedules of her activity; a second dean spent 21.7 per cent of her time in this way; a third, 29 per cent; a fourth, 26 per cent, etc. The average per cent of time spent by these 14 deans in performing this duty was 24.2 per cent, etc.

one dean spent 56 per cent of her time in the personal advisement of pupils, and 6 per cent in the control of the intellectual environment; while another spent 17 per cent of her time in personal advisement, and 33 per cent in the control of the intellectual environment. One dean spent only 3 per cent of her time on group activities of pupils, and 20 per cent in managing her office.* These differences in emphasis are due to many factors, some of which are the size and location of the school, the character and needs of the pupils, the attitude of the principal and teachers regarding the dean's work, the dean's staff, the interests and abilities of members of the school staff, the personality and interests of the dean herself, and her vision of the possibilities of her position.

NIGHT WORK DONE BY DEANS

Three-fourths of these hundred deans reported that their position required night work of two kinds—attending school functions and preparing for the next day's work. The school functions most frequently mentioned were social events, athletic contests, rehearsals of plays, and meetings of other extra-curriculum activities. Chaperoning these events is specifically mentioned twenty times.

The types of preparation which occupy part of the evenings of these deans are: Making plans, writing bulletins and notices, reading professional magazines and books relating to their work, composing speeches, doing clerical work, and attending to correspondence.

Five deans reported visiting the homes of pupils in the evening.

Thirteen deans stated that they performed no professional duties at night. Twelve did not answer this question. Size of school does not seem to be a factor in determining the amount of evening work which deans do.

OFFICE HOURS OF DEANS

Three-fourths of the eighty-seven deans reporting on this question have stated office hours; the others do not. Of these, thirty are available in their offices the entire school day of 6 to 7 hours; seven, from 5 to 6 hours; seventeen, from 4 to 5 hours; five, from 3 to 4 hours; thirteen, from 2 to 3 hours; eight, from 1 to 2 hours; and seven, less than 1 hour. Ten deans reserve one hour in

* Similar extreme variations may be noted in Table XV in the activities of deans in smaller schools also.

the morning and one in the afternoon as office hours; sixteen keep two hours free for conferences during both sessions; four reserve two hours in the morning and the entire afternoon. Where the dean carries a teaching program, her office hours would of course be limited by that fact. In the schools enrolling more than a thousand pupils, the dean is in her office practically the entire school day. Doubtless the dean should be readily available to pupils, but the question arises as to whether an efficient time budget should not provide some uninterrupted time for making plans and studying special problems.

EXTENSION OF THE DEAN'S WORK

To the question, "Will you give us an idea of any work which you feel you should and could handle, but of which you do not have charge at present?" twenty-six deans made no reply; seven said "none"; six remarked that they had no time for additional duties; and three said that they had too much to do now and wished to drop some of their responsibilities, rather than to add other obligations.

Fifteen deans felt that they could and should extend their work with the social program and with other group activities of pupils. Four wished to have charge of the social calendar. One, however, stated that she "preferred administrative and executive to social work."

Four would like to devote more energy to the health program.

Nine deans evinced interest in the academic phases of their work such as the making of pupils' program, advisement of pupils who are failing, and general educational advisement.

Three deans would like to give an orientation course for girls entering the school—"social as well as academic orientation."

While many deans are trying to delegate the duty of giving excuses for absence and tardiness to some one else, two deans wished to assume this responsibility.

Two deans would like to have a share in revising the curriculum. The supervision of girls living away from home, closer contact with home-room teachers, supervision of the student council, participation in assemblies, and the giving of a vocational guidance course were mentioned by one or two deans as duties which they could and should perform.

Six deans spoke with appreciation of the freedom given them

to develop the position as they desired. One said she was "given a free hand"; another that she was "never barred from doing anything that she wanted to do." Apparently limitations of time frequently deterred deans from expanding their work.

Summary

Judging from the replies of one hundred selected deans and the daily schedules of twenty-one, we may conclude that the duties which take the largest amount of their time are those relating to the personal advisement and group activities of pupils.

The five main phases of work with individuals listed in the order of frequency with which each is performed are: (1) Interviewing pupils who come voluntarily with personal problems; (2) interviewing pupils referred to the dean by other members of the faculty; (3) discovering cases of maladjustment; (4) following up cases of maladjustment; and (5) pursuing a systematic plan of educational and vocational guidance. The personal problems with which the dean frequently deals relate to study, health, social adjustments at school and at home, conduct, financial difficulties and employment.

The five main phases of work with groups are: (1) Attending social events and meetings of extra-curriculum activities; (2) conferring with committees of pupils and with officers of clubs; (3) conferring with sponsors of girls' organizations; (4) initiating new activities to meet the needs of different groups; and (5) addressing or securing speakers to address groups of girls.

Five other phases of the dean's work which are equally important, though in general less time-consuming are: (1) The general supervision of the physical and social aspects of the school environment; (2) the control of the intellectual environment by assisting the principal and faculty in the making of academic policies and in helping students to select and succeed in courses suited to their capacity; (3) the extension of influence and the creation of good will through informal contacts with pupils, teachers, parents, and visitors; (4) the routine duties relating to the office itself; and (5) the individual study and association with professional people necessary to keep in touch with new developments in the field.

Two prominent features of the work of these 100 deans were the extreme variation in the amount of time spent in different duties and the marked coöperation of the dean with others.

CHAPTER VI

DETAILED DESCRIPTION OF THE MAJOR DIVISIONS OF THE DEAN'S WORK

After obtaining a general view of the duties which the majority of these hundred deans perform, those to which they devote the largest amount of their time and those which they think properly belong to the dean's office, the reader may be interested in viewing more closely each phase of personnel work in high school, and the relation of the dean and other members of the staff to each aspect.

PERSONAL ADVISEMENT OF GIRLS

Personal advisement is the phase of work with individuals which is performed most frequently by deans, which consumes the largest amount of their time, and which, in their opinion, should be one of their functions.

Personal advisement includes the prevention and treatment of all kinds of maladjustment—physical, educational, social, vocational, and economic. The dean's part in this program is fivefold: (1) To interview freshmen early in the year; (2) to interview girls who come to her voluntarily with personal problems of all kinds; (3) to interview girls referred to her by other members of the school; (4) to discover and follow up cases of maladjustment; and (5) to give systematically vocational and educational guidance.

The problem of counseling girls is a very difficult and precarious one involving great responsibility. There are certain questions, such as "What are the entrance requirements of Smith College?" to which the dean can give a certain and definite answer. There are others as to how to cure a long standing cold, or what vocation one should enter which should be referred to a specialist. This distinction in types of advice and kinds of interviews must be kept clearly in mind in interpreting data on the dean's function in interviewing girls.

Interviewing Freshmen. In seventy schools the deans reported that they interview every freshman girl early in the year. From the standpoint of the early detection and prevention of maladjustment and the prompt and happy adjustment of girls to high school, this is an important duty. It is performed by:

(*a*) The dean alone in 30, or 43 per cent, of the schools performing the function to any extent;

(*b*) The dean in coöperation with others in 14, or 20 per cent, of the schools;

(*c*) Some one else in 25, or 36 per cent, of the schools.

In the smallest schools (enrollment of 250-499) the "some one else" is usually the principal. In the next largest group, teachers and vice-principal as well as the principal perform this function either alone or in coöperation with the dean. In one school enrolling 575 pupils, the dean is assisted in interviewing freshmen by two or three teachers and the principal. In another school of 607 pupils there is a special freshman adviser who coöperates with the dean in interviewing freshmen.

In the schools enrolling more than a thousand pupils the advisers and home-room teachers usually interview freshmen. In several cases a special officer, such as the registrar, educational counselor, or vocational guidance counselor, helps freshmen to adjust to their new school environment. In a school with an enrollment of 1,638 pupils, each girl planning to enter high school has a short conference with the high school dean after she makes out her program with the junior high school adviser.

The size of the school does not seem to determine whether or not the dean performs this duty. In the larger, as well as in the smaller, schools, approximately one-third of the deans interview freshmen early in the year. This similarity among schools of different sizes may be due to quite different factors. In the small schools the dean may feel that there is less need for her to interview systematically every freshman; while in the large schools the number of pupils makes it physically impossible for the dean alone to do this work thoroughly. The dean in large schools, however, can help the home-room teacher or grade advisers in making their interviews with freshmen effective and valuable.

Further investigation would doubtless show wide variation in the quality of these interviews, some being merely perfunctory, and others resulting in a friendly relationship between the girl and her adviser. In these interviews with freshmen, the dean may obtain a nucleus of information essential in helping each individual to profit most fully by her experience in high school.

Interviewing Girls Who Come Voluntarily with Personal Problems. Information was obtained from the questionnaires concerning the dean's relation to problems of study, health, financial difficulties, home difficulties, personal problems of a social nature, and employment.[1]

In all the schools, as might be expected, some one interviews girls who recognize their *study difficulties* and seek advice concerning them. This duty is reported to be performed by:

(*a*) the dean alone in 24, or 24 per cent, of the schools;
(*b*) the dean in coöperation with others in 66, or 66 per cent, of the schools;
(*c*) other people in 5, or 5 per cent, of the schools.

In the smallest schools the dean usually coöperates with the principal in performing this duty; less frequently with classroom teachers and home-room teachers. As the schools increase in size, the principal is consulted less, and the teachers and advisers more often. In schools enrolling more than one thousand pupils, the registrar and heads of department occasionally counsel girls in regard to study problems.

In the larger as well as the smaller schools, girls come to the deans with study difficulties in approximately two-thirds of the schools in each group. There are certain phases of study problems with which the dean can advantageously assist the classroom teachers and home-room teachers who sometimes do not appreciate the influence which emotional, social, and physical factors exert upon academic achievement. In 64, or 67 per cent, of the schools the dean coöperates with others in this phase of advisory work.

Health is another personal problem with which practically all the schools are concerned. In very few cases does the dean interview girls who come to her with health problems without seeking the assistance of some other member of the staff. In the smaller schools the nurse is the specialist to whom pupils are usually

[1] In some cases the dean stated that a given duty was performed in the school but did not designate by whom it was performed. These percentages, accordingly, do not total 100. Anyone who is interested, can easily estimate the number of deans who did not reply to a given question.

referred. In schools having no nurse, the principal or physical education teacher is consulted. In the larger schools the physical education department and the doctor play an increasingly prominent rôle. In four schools a health education department gives health counsel to pupils.

Emergency cases of illness are handled by:

(*a*) the dean in 35, or 37 per cent, of the schools;
(*b*) the dean in coöperation with the doctor, nurse, matron, physical education, or health education department in 40, or 42 per cent, of the schools;
(*c*) some one besides the dean in 20, or 21 per cent, of the schools.

In schools which have no full-time nurse, the dean's office is frequently the only place to which emergency cases of illness can be sent. In schools having a nurse, the dean is often asked to make necessary school adjustments for the pupil and to get in touch with her home. Forty-nine deans think they should not have sole responsibility for emergency cases of illness, even though lack of health facilities makes it necessary for them to perform this duty at present; eleven claimed no responsibility for the dean in this matter; the rest did not answer the question.

Financial problems are dealt with in 95 per cent of the schools. Girls come with these problems to:

(*a*) the dean alone in 43, or 45 per cent, of the schools;
(*b*) the dean in coöperation with others in 45, or 47 per cent, of the schools;
(*c*) some other person in 4, or 4 per cent, of the schools.

As in the case of other personal problems, the principal in the smaller schools is consulted. In the larger schools the advisers, teachers, and special officers or committees, such as the vocational guidance director and the student loan committee, interview pupils who seek help in financial matters. Without the assistance of outside agencies or scholarship and loan committees, it seems that the dean's interview would frequently end at the point at which real assistance might be given.

Difficulties at home are frequently found to underlie many problems. Interviewing girls concerning family relationships is a duty performed in 97 per cent of the schools by:

(*a*) the dean alone in 47, or 48 per cent, of these schools;

(*b*) the dean in coöperation with others in 45, or 46 per cent, of the schools;

(*c*) other people in 3, or 3 per cent, of the schools.

The "other people" consulted are the principal in the group of smallest schools; and advisers, home-room teachers, vocational counselor, visiting teachers, and home visitor in other schools.

Ninety-seven per cent of the schools are interested in the *social problems* of individuals. Girls who voluntarily seek guidance in this type of problem consult:

(*a*) the dean alone in 52, or 54 per cent, of the schools;

(*b*) the dean and others in 42, or 43 per cent, of the schools;

(*c*) other people only, in none of these schools.

The same individuals coöperate with the dean in this as in the preceding problem, and no significant difference due to size of school was found.

Ninety-seven per cent of the schools assist pupils in finding *employment*. This duty is performed by:

(*a*) the dean alone in 36, or 37 per cent, of the schools;

(*b*) the dean in coöperation with others in 46, or 47 per cent, of the schools;

(*c*) other officers in 13, or 13 per cent, of the schools.

In schools enrolling less than 500 pupils the principal usually assists pupils in finding employment. In the larger schools special departments assume the major part of the responsibility. In schools having an enrollment of more than one thousand girls the commercial department handles this phase of guidance in two cases, while fourteen schools report having a special employment bureau or vocational guidance director.

Interviewing Girls Who Are Referred to the Dean by Other Members of the School. In addition to the girls who come to the dean with their problems, there are those pupils whose problems are obvious to others though perhaps not to the girls themselves. These girls are frequently referred to the dean. One dean of 5,000 girls writes concerning her policy: "When a girl is sent to me, I take up all possible aspects of her needs, using all facilities of the school and available social agencies useful for her adjustment."

Girls failing in their academic work are interviewed by some one in 96 per cent of the schools. They are referred to:

(*a*) the dean in 31, or 32 per cent, of the schools;
(*b*) the dean and others in 56, or 58 per cent, of the schools;
(*c*) other people in 8, or 8 per cent, of the schools.

In the group of smallest schools the principal invariably performs this function in coöperation with the dean. In the larger schools the classroom teachers, home-room teachers, and advisers assume this responsibility. In one school having a total enrollment of 720 pupils, "every teacher is given the names of a few pupils who are failing or are very low in academic work. It is his duty to confer with these students and their teachers once a week, and report concerning their progress to the office of the assistant principal and dean of girls, who make further investigation." In schools so large that the dean cannot personally interview all students who are working below their capacity, an important part of her work consists in helping classroom teachers and home-room teachers to do this work better than they otherwise could.

In the case of *health* problems referred to the dean, the situation is similar to that described in a previous paragraph regarding health problems brought to her voluntarily by girls. In 59 per cent of the schools the dean works with the nurse, doctor, advisers, physical education department, and teachers in any way in which she can be of assistance.

The problem of *absence and tardiness* is recognized in all schools and has two aspects—the routine administrative and the personal aspects. In 522 representative secondary schools[2] reports of absence and tardiness are summarized, and admission slips issued by the principal, assistant principal, teacher, attendance secretary, information clerk, or pupil assistant. This phase of dealing with absence and tardiness is not one of the dean's duties. It is the personal aspect with which the dean is concerned. Interviewing girls referred because of absence and tardiness enables the dean to make personal contacts with pupils, teachers, and parents, and frequently to discover cases of maladjustment which might otherwise pass unnoticed.

In 26, or 29 per cent, of the schools, the dean alone interviews girls concerning absence and tardiness in practically all cases; in 14, or 16 per cent, of the schools she coöperates with others in this matter, and in 44, or 49 per cent, of the schools some

[2] Woellner, Robert and Reavis, W. C., "Administrative Practices in Dealing with Personnel Problems in Secondary Schools," *The School Review,* 37: pp. 177-179, March, 1929.

one else does this work. In exceptional cases, however, the dean assumes more responsibility for this work both alone and in coöperation with others.

In the smaller schools the principal and dean investigate cases of absence and tardiness. In fourteen of the schools enrolling more than 1,000 pupils, an attendance clerk is in charge of the routine phases of this work. In one school enrolling 2,239 pupils the vice-principal issues admittance and tardy slips to absentees and tardy pupils and summarizes attendance. Unexcused absentees are the only ones who are really interviewed. An office helper calls up the home of each absentee on the first day of absence. The assistant principal in fourteen schools relieves the dean and principal of this duty. An attendance officer is called upon in four cases. In schools of all sizes practically all the deans investigate exceptional cases of absence and tardiness either alone or in coöperation with others. In only 29 per cent of the schools do they interview *all* girls who are absent or tardy.

Discipline is another problem common to all schools at the present time. Although theoretically it should be possible to prevent most misconduct, by adapting the school environment to the interests and capacity of every pupil, practice is behind the theory, and misbehavior does occur. Woellner and Reavis,[3] in their study of 522 representative schools, found that unruly pupils were sent to the principal's office in 91.6 per cent of the schools.

In the hundred selected schools in this study cases of misconduct among girls are referred to:

(*a*) the dean in 26, or 29 per cent, of the schools;
(*b*) the dean in coöperation with others in 17, or 19 per cent, of the schools;
(*c*) some one else in 42, or 46 per cent, of the schools.

In the smallest schools, again the "some one else" is usually the principal. In the larger schools the principal and the assistant principal still hold first place as disciplinary officers, although the dean in these schools frequently confers with teachers and advisers concerning the conduct of girls. In schools enrolling more than a thousand girls only eight deans report having responsibility for practically all cases of misconduct among girls.

A larger number of deans (46 per cent) report that they coöperate with the principal, assistant principal, and teachers in

[3] Woellner, Robert and Reavis, W. C., *op. cit.*, p. 181.

dealing with *exceptional* cases of misconduct among girls. If discipline cases are considered as a type of maladjustment which requires constructive remedial treatment rather than as a perverse disregard for authority, the dean's office should be concerned with these as well as with other serious problem cases that are referred to her.

Discovering Cases of Maladjustment. In addition to interviewing girls who come voluntarily or are referred by other members of the school, the dean should also try to discover cases of maladjustment before they become so serious that they demand her attention. The girls who overtly break rules and defy authority are promptly brought to the proper authority; but psychiatrists state that this type of conduct is not so serious as a more introvert kind of maladjustment which is less frequently detected. Dull girls unable to do high school work, to be sure, are usually discovered early in their high school career; but superior girls who are doing merely average work or work below average still frequently pass through high school unnoticed and unstimulated to develop to their maximum capacity. Unsocial girls, over-social girls, girls having trouble at home, and girls below par in health represent other types of maladjustment which are frequently neglected because they do not come to the attention of the person who is best fitted to help them. This preventive phase of advisory work is apparently not performed at all in from 10 to 23 per cent of the schools.

The dean alone does very little in the discovery of intellectually superior and inferior pupils, although she coöperates with others in approximately 50, or 58 per cent, of the schools reporting. In schools of all sizes, the classroom teachers, home-room teachers, and advisers aid the dean in performing this duty. In four schools having an enrollment of more than 1,000 pupils the psychology department, which has the technique and knowledge necessary to discover and guide exceptional children, relieves the dean of responsibility in this matter. The vocational guidance department or committee also coöperate in the discovery of this type of problem. In the majority of schools, however, the teachers can best detect these cases and refer them to the person best fitted to advise. The dean encourages teachers to find pupils who need individual attention and to refer them to the proper authority.

Social maladjustments are discovered by:

(*a*) the dean in 41, or 45 per cent, of the schools;

(*b*) the dean in coöperation with others in 44, or 48 per cent, of the schools;

(*c*) other people in 3, or 3 per cent, of the schools.

In this case also, the coöperation of the dean with the teachers is essential. In schools having an enrollment of more than 1,000 girls, the dean is aided in this phase of her work by the psychology department, visiting teachers, and "Big Sisters," as well as by the teachers and advisers.

In the discovery, as in the treatment of health problems, the dean's rôle is largely one of aiding and coördinating, in whatever way she can, the work of the nurse, doctor, health department, physical education teachers, or other persons especially interested in the health of pupils.

Following-up Cases of Maladjustment. The discovery of problems which need attention is of little value unless the case is followed to a satisfactory solution. Not more than 70 per cent of the schools reported work along this line. Of this number many felt that the work they were doing was entirely inadequate. In approximately half of the schools the dean reports that she is responsible for the follow-up of intellectual and social problems; in a still smaller number of schools does she have assistance in this work. Other persons are assigned to this duty in fewer than ten schools. In seven of the largest schools, a visiting teacher, vocational guidance director, outside social agency, or social worker in the school does some of this necessary case work more thoroughly than the dean with her limitations of time and special training could do it. Health problems seem to be more thoroughly followed up by the dean, the nurse, the doctor, the physical education and health departments, and visiting teachers than any other type of problem. Although deans recognize the importance of making complete case studies of individuals, according to their own statements, there are very few who have as yet mastered the technique, or have sufficient time and assistance to perform this function. In a school in New York City having an enrollment of approximately 5,000 girls, "case records are kept:

(*a*) by the dean of all cases with which she deals, and of all cases given psychiatric care;

(*b*) by the psychologist of all individual psychological examinations. These are filed in the vocational counselors' and the deans' offices."

Cases of illness are followed up by:

(*a*) the dean in 23, or 28 per cent, of the 83 schools in which this work is done;

(*b*) the dean in coöperation with the nurse, doctor, attendance officer, physical education department or visiting teacher, in 34, or 41 per cent, of the schools;

(*c*) one of these special officers or departments, without assistance from the dean in 25, or 30 per cent, of the schools.

The differences in practice in the care of cases of illness in these 100 high schools, as indicated in this study, are no doubt correlated with the differences in the organization and kind of positive health programs in the schools, and with the preparation of the dean along health lines.

Giving Vocational Guidance. Almost one-third of these deans give vocational guidance in the 85 per cent of the schools in which this function is reported. It is performed by:

(*a*) the dean alone in 25, or 29 per cent, of the schools;

(*b*) the dean, in coöperation with others, in 46, or 54 per cent, of the schools;

(*c*) some one else in 12, or 14 per cent, of the schools reporting.

One-third of these deans stated positively that they do not think vocational guidance is a duty for which the dean should be responsible. To help pupils choose, prepare for, and enter a vocation requires specialized knowledge of vocations and of individuals, and special techniques. It demands time for investigating industrial conditions as well as for interviewing pupils and employers. Should not this function be performed, as it is at present in some of the larger schools, by a vocational guidance director? The dean's rôle in this as in so many other phases of her work is to meet the exigencies of the present situation as well as possible. She can do this by contributing information about individual pupils and positions to the vocational guidance bureau in schools having such a bureau. In schools having no specialist in charge of vocational guidance and placement, the dean can and does interview pupils who come to her for advice, makes available appropriate reading material about occupations for women, investigates suitable and safe opportunities for employment for girls who need to earn money, and establishes contacts between pupils and people who are successfully engaged in occupations in which the girls are interested.

Opportunities for employment for girls are investigated by:

(*a*) The dean in 34, or 41 per cent, of the 82 schools performing this function;

(*b*) the dean in coöperation with others in 27, or 33 per cent, of the schools;

(*c*) some other person in 18, or 22 per cent, of the schools.

The situation in regard to approving conditions under which girls work is similar to that of finding suitable positions, except that the dean less frequently coöperates with others in this task. In 32, or 39 per cent, of the 81 schools reporting, some one else, usually the commercial department and the principal in the smaller schools, and the commercial department, employment bureau, and vocational guidance director in the larger schools—assist girls in securing positions after graduation.

Twenty of the larger schools report having an employment bureau or a vocational guidance department. In the smaller schools the commercial department most frequently assumes responsibility for placement. In the schools enrolling fewer than 1,000 pupils, the principal, teachers, and advisers give vocational guidance, probably of an incidental and unscientific kind. All of these persons possess information about pupils which is useful in helping them to choose a vocation and to obtain suitable preparation for it, but it is unlikely that any of them have sufficient time to devote to the study of vocations. Neither are they likely to have a scientific knowledge of the needs of the individuals whom they are attempting to advise. Consequently it is doubtful if they are qualified to give effective guidance.

If the dean, however, has specialized in vocational guidance, she might well make this a central feature of her work through which she approaches problems of other kinds. That the vocational approach to personal problems is psychologically sound is indicated by the fact that pupils are keenly cognizant of the vocational objective of education.[4]

[4] Thomson, Lyle G., "Objectives of Secondary Education According to the Opinions of Pupils," *The School Review*, 37:198-203, March, 1929.

Giving Educational Guidance. In nearly one-fourth of the hundred schools the dean is primarily responsible for the educational guidance of pupils. Girls are officially assisted in making their programs by:

(*a*) the dean in 22, or 24 per cent, of the cases;

(*b*) the dean in coöperation with others in 36, or 39 per cent, of the schools;

(*c*) some one else in 34, or 37 per cent, of the schools.

In the smaller schools the "some one else" is, as usual, the principal; in the schools enrolling more than 1,000 pupils, the home-room teachers, advisers, and assistant principal most often perform this function. In three schools having an enrollment of more than 1,000 girls, the vocational guidance department gives educational guidance also. Ten deans in the two groups of larger schools are officially responsible for helping the girls to make their programs, but thirty-nine definitely state that the dean should not perform this duty alone. The majority of deans, however, advise girls unofficially concerning their academic programs. A dean who knows a pupil intimately and has made an intensive study of opportunities in higher education can frequently give a pupil a long-distance view of her educational career which an adviser, interested chiefly in the immediate choice of studies, may have neglected.

Administering Loans and Scholarships. Seventy per cent of the schools report having loan or scholarship funds. These funds are administered by:

(*a*) the dean in 23, or 33 per cent, of the schools;

(*b*) the dean and others in 29, or 41 per cent, of the schools;

(*c*) other people in 17, or 24 per cent, of the schools.

It is usually the principal or a committee who administers loans and scholarships in schools of all sizes.

The group of schools enrolling fewer than 500 pupils differs from the other groups in less frequently having loan and scholarship funds.

A number of deans have initiated and secured contributions for scholarship funds, which enable them to give the needed practical assistance which their conferences with individuals has revealed.

Summary and Discussion. The outstanding feature in the advisory work of these deans is the function of coördinating the many services offered by the school for the welfare of the girl. For example, in the case of students failing in academic work, parents, classroom teachers, doctor, and psychologist combine with the dean, as specialists do in a clinic, to deal scientifically with the problem. One dean writes: "I cannot think of any interview which would end with me alone. I would need help from all sources."

Two different practices may be noted in regard to the delegation of these advisory duties. In some schools "any one knowing the situation" is expected to give advice in a given case; in other schools, one person is definitely assigned to a particular phase of advisory work. The point of view of one dean is sound: "If there is some one in the school who can help a girl better than the dean, the girl should of course go to that person." In fact, one of the most important duties of the dean in a large school is to discover teachers having special aptitude and interest in various phases of advisory work. Their specialized knowledge will enable the dean to induct them into the work.

Another aspect of the dean's advisory work is the education of all the teachers in regard to their opportunities and responsibilities in recognizing problem cases, referring them to the dean or other person best qualified to deal with them, and in sending to the dean's office, and receiving from the dean's office information about individuals useful in giving practical constructive advice. One dean wrote: "The teachers are not yet accustomed to having someone to whom they may refer cases of these kinds."

The amount of personal advice which these deans give is large. Further investigations are needed to describe and perhaps improve its quality. Much of the time spent in advising pupils may be wasted, because the dean has not acquired, either the necessary facts concerning the problem, the individual, and the relation of the individual to the problem, or the technique of presenting the facts effectively.

There is a real need for objective measures of the effect of interviews, the analysis of the methods used by skilled interviewers, and the compilation of knowledge needed in solving each specific kind of problem.

GROUP ACTIVITIES OF GIRLS

The dean's work with groups of girls is as important as her work with individuals. The aim of both of these phases of her work is the same, namely, the growth and development of each pupil. The amount of time devoted to work with groups and to work with individuals must be nicely balanced. In fact, one of the dean's problems is to discover the extent to which she can work effectively with individuals in groups as well as in personal interviews. The group activities which the dean encourages should prevent the occurrence of some of the problems requiring individual treatment.

Orientation of Freshmen. In larger schools the dean may save time in the interviews with freshmen by giving in group meetings information needed by all entering pupils. This duty is performed to some extent in 88 schools. The persons in charge of this work are:

(*a*) the dean in 26, or 30 per cent, of the schools;

(*b*) the dean in coöperation with others in 47, or 53 per cent, of the schools;

(*c*) some one else in 15, or 17 per cent, of the schools.

In all except the group of largest schools the principal is mentioned in connection with this duty. Advisers and home-room teachers play a prominent part in schools of all sizes, as do also the student council and "Big Sisters," under the direction of the dean.

Opportunities for freshmen to become acquainted with the faculty and fellow pupils are arranged by essentially the same people who assist in the more official phases of orientation.

Directing Social Life and Extra-curriculum Activities. The coöperative aspect of this function is vividly shown by the answers to the specific questions regarding this phase of the dean's work. The constructive educational way in which deans are performing this duty is also revealed.

Meetings of many of the extra-curriculum activities are attended by:

(*a*) the dean alone in 38, or 40 per cent, of the 94 schools reporting;

(*b*) the dean in coöperation with others in 50, or 53 per cent, of the schools;

(*c*) other people in 5, or 5 per cent, of the schools.

Supervision of extra-curriculum activities apparently requires that the dean attend in person many of the meetings. This is especially necessary when the dean is readjusting the social program or initiating new activities. Her rôle is one of friendly visitor or invited guest; not of chaperon, or critic, or "supervisor." Only 19 per cent of these deans serve as sole chaperon of school affairs. Half of them stated positively that in their opinion the dean should not be required personally to chaperon school affairs. In 58 per cent of the cases they are assisted by teachers, principal, parents, advisers, and club sponsors. In 18 per cent of the schools the dean delegates this duty to some one else.

Thirty-nine, or 46 per cent, of these deans reported that they are primarily responsible for initiating new activities; forty-one, or 49 per cent, mention assistance from teachers, sponsors, principal, and pupils in organizing new clubs for which there seems to be a need.

Approximately the same proportion of deans regulates participation in extra-curriculum activities. The prominent part which students play in operating the point system is interesting.

The dean has charge of the social calendar in approximately half of the schools; the principal, in almost one-fifth of the schools; and the dean, in coöperation with principal, advisers, or teachers, in almost one-third of the schools. Rather curiously, twenty deans said that this should not be their responsibility. Theoretically, the dean, one of whose two chief duties is the supervision of the social program of the whole school, seems to be the most logical person to have charge of the social calendar. Such an arrangement helps to prevent conflicts in the dates of social events.

Sixty schools reported having an "All Girls" organization. In 40, or 67 per cent, of these cases, this organization was personally supervised by the dean; rarely by some other person.

A larger number of schools, eighty-two, have student government associations. This activity is personally supervised by:

(*a*) the dean in only 14, or 17 per cent, of the schools;

(*b*) the dean, with others, in 29, or 35 per cent, of the schools;

(*c*) the principal, teachers, advisers, student council or committee in 36, or 44 per cent, of the schools.

Forty-five deans believe that this function should not belong primarily to them. In schools of all sizes, the principal plays the most prominent part in this phase of student life.

The financial aspects of girls' organizations are supervised by:

(*a*) the dean in 24, or 28 per cent, of the schools;

(*b*) the dean in coöperation with others in 28, or 33 per cent, of the schools;

(*c*) the principal, commercial department, advisers, or school treasurer in 29, or 34 per cent, of the schools.

The forty deans who said that this should not be the dean's function probably feel that a person specially appointed to serve as school treasurer can perform this duty with greater economy of time and effort than they can.

The constructive work which these deans are doing is suggested by the large number who work with committees of girls in planning social events and with officers and committees of girls' organizations.

Eighty-eight deans, alone or with advisers, sponsors, and teachers, assist girls in planning school affairs. Seventy-nine deans reported similar conferences with officers and committees of girls' organizations. Three-fourths of the hundred deans stated positively their opinion of the real value of this part of their work. Coöperating with students in this way not only relieves the dean of much direct supervision, but also helps to develop leadership, coöperation, and responsibility on the part of the pupils.

The same number confer with sponsors of girls' clubs. As schools increase in size the dean must extend her influence on individual pupils more and more through the sponsors of clubs, teachers, and advisers who have direct contact with the pupils. Practically all of the deans in schools of all sizes recognize the importance of this work with club leaders in achieving the maximum educational values of the activities program.

Approximately three-fourths of the schools report some social service emphasis in the social program of the school. Sixty-four deans, either alone or in coöperation with advisers, Girl Reserves, principal, social workers, or the Girls' League, try to arrange opportunities for girls to engage in social service.

Another way in which the dean can exert influence on groups of students is by addressing large or small groups of girls, and by securing speakers to address them. That this is an important part of her work is shown by the large number of deans, eighty-one, who perform this duty. They are frequently assisted by the principal, advisers, teachers, and committees of students. Small informal discussion groups have been found to be an excellent way to build desirable attitudes on many questions.

Very few deans systematically keep in touch with alumnae; very many would like to do so. Sixty-three deans reported that they have incidental contacts with alumnae. The principal, assistant principal, and teachers also meet former pupils in an informal way. Two deans mentioned the existence of alumnae associations, and three referred to the school paper as a factor in continuing contacts with pupils who have graduated. Interviews with former pupils are an important means by which the dean can check the long-distance effect of her advisory work, and can ascertain the features of her program which girls have found helpful and the deficiencies in their education which she may be able to prevent in future classes.

Summary and Discussion. As previous studies have shown, the supervision of group activities is one of the dean's major functions. She frequently attends club meetings and social events as a guest and interested observer rather than as a chaperon and critic. She personally supervises the Girls' League in the majority of schools in which this organization exists, but is not so often primarily responsible for the oversight of student government. One of the most constructive features of the dean's direction of the social life of the school is her conferences with sponsors of clubs and with committees of pupils and pupil officers. Through these individuals the dean can indirectly reach the entire student body, and at the same time give these teachers and pupils a practical course in the management of student organizations and social events.

CONTROL OF THE SCHOOL ENVIRONMENT

The sanitary and social aspects of the school building exert their influence silently on all the pupils all of the time. The custodian of the building is primarily responsible for the physical condition of the building, but the dean, principal, nurse, and teachers notice unsatisfactory conditions and report them to the proper authorities. In four schools, committees of students systematically inspect the building; in two schools, the health education department considers this one of its functions. As is the case with other duties, the supervision of the sanitary condition of the school building is not one of the dean's functions, but is one that many deans perform as need arises.

The health equipment—rest room, first aid material, etc.—is supervised by:

(*a*) the dean in 30 of the 100 schools;
(*b*) the dean in coöperation with others in 36 schools;
(*c*) the nurse, doctor, physical education, health, home economics departments, or the Boy Scouts in 32 schools.

The social aspects of the environment, such as loitering in the halls, conduct in the cafeteria, etc., are supervised by:

(*a*) the dean in 15 of the 98 schools reporting;
(*b*) the dean in coöperation with others in 59 schools;
(*c*) some one else in 24 schools.

In schools having 250-1,000 pupils, the principal and teachers have the most prominent share in this duty. In schools enrolling more than one thousand pupils, members of the student council, or a committee of students, have taken charge of this work, and, in some of the schools visited, were doing it in an effective and educational way.

CONTROL OF THE INTELLECTUAL ENVIRONMENT

The intellectual life of high school pupils is influenced noticeably by the classroom instruction, study habits, the home-room period, the courses offered, the clearness with which the aims of the school and the means by which pupils can profit by their opportunities are presented, the assembly periods, the provision of worthwhile, interesting reading material, and the study of the mental abilities of each individual.

Classroom Instruction. In the classes which the dean herself teaches, she has the opportunity to use the best methods of instruction. It will be seen from Table XVI that thirty-six deans do not teach at all, while others teach 22 hours, the mean for all groups being 7.4 hours per week. Sixty-four of these hundred deans teach from 5 to 22 hours a week; seventeen, 1 period a day; twelve, 2 periods; seventeen, 3 periods; and six, 6 periods.

The dean may also influence methods of instruction, entrance requirements, and the curriculum, through faculty meetings and conferences and committee meetings with faculty and principal in which school policies are formed. The deans in eighty-five schools reported that they assist in policy-making regarding these matters. In thirty-five of the schools, the dean has a voice in the selection of the faculty, and thus indirectly may influence instruction.

Home-Room Responsibilities. Only eight of these deans have charge of a home-room. This part of the school program is plainly not one of the dean's duties, nor do they think it should be.

TABLE XVI

TEACHING LOAD OF DEANS OF GIRLS IN HIGH SCHOOL

(*100 Selected Deans*)

	NUMBER OF HOURS OF TEACHING PER WEEK				
	Group I	Group II	Group III	Group IV	Total (All Groups)
Lowest	15	0	0	0	0
Q_1	14.80	1.81	1.19	0.93	1.39
Median	16.00	11.00	4.56	1.87	5.65
Q_3	20.00	15.19	6.50	8.00	14.35
Highest	20	20	22	15	22
Number doing no teaching	0	8	13	15	36
Mean	16.74	9.45	5.03	3.95	7.41
S. D.	2.44	4.04	2.98	2.88	6.76
Number of cases ...	12	29	31	28	100

This table is read as follows: In the 12 schools in Group I, the lowest number of hours which any dean teaches is 15; the highest, 20; the median, 16. One-fourth of the deans teach less than 14.8 hours; three-fourths teach less than 20 hours. Everyone of these deans teaches. The arithmetical mean is 16.74 hours, and the standard deviation is 2.44, etc.

Intellectual Orientation of Pupils. Half of the schools reported some attempt to orient pupils to the school and to life, in those matters concerning their academic progress. In these schools the duty is performed by:

(a) the dean in 33, or 65 per cent, of the cases;

(b) the dean in coöperation with principal, advisers, home-room teachers, psychology department or special education counselor in 12, or 23 per cent, of the schools;

(c) one of these other officers without the dean in 7, or 13 per cent, of the schools.

Although each period brings its own unique problems, orientation of freshmen and intellectual guidance of boys and girls during their period of transition from *pupil* to *student* are perhaps more necessary than the orientation of college students. In fact, if pupils during their four years of secondary school acquired effective habits of study and grew in the power to solve their own problems, as they arose, much less "orientation" of college students might be necessary.

Seventy-nine schools reported efforts to teach pupils how to study. This duty is performed by:

(a) the dean in 10, or 13 per cent, of the schools;

(b) the dean in coöperation with others in 29, or 37 per cent, of the schools.

(c) the classroom teacher, home-room teacher, adviser, principal, or vocational guidance department in 37, or 47 per cent, of the schools.

There are many phases of the "how to study" problem which come to the dean's attention in interviews on personal problems. Some call for better instruction in methods of study, others for better assignment procedures, others for better grouping of pupils according to their abilities, still others for better home conditions where emotional, financial, or other difficulties are interfering with academic achievement. The discovery of these environmental hindrances to good study habits is the first step in an attempt to correct them.

Attending Assembly. In ninety-four of the schools the deans attend assembly periods. Through their interest in and help on the programs presented in the assembly periods, they may have a direct influence on the intellectual environment of the school.

Provision of Worthwhile Books and Magazines. An important part of the intellectual environment of high school pupils is the books and magazines available for them to read in their leisure time. The responsibility for directing pupils' reading usually rests upon the librarian. Thirty-eight deans, however, reported that they encourage reading as a leisure activity by coöperating with the librarian and by providing additional books, magazines, and clippings of interest to pupils. One dean, for example, has placed on a table in her office some interesting articles and books relating to vocations for women.

Study of Academic Achievement of Individual Pupils. Practically all these deans are consulted by teachers, advisers, and principals concerning the academic work of girls. Sometimes the dean, in connection with another problem, wishes to ascertain from teachers the academic achievement of a particular pupil. Frequently teachers, advisers, and principal desire personal data from the dean about a girl who is failing in her studies. These conferences with principal and teachers concerning the academic work of pupils, reported by ninety-three of the deans, should result in a better understanding of the scholastic difficulties of pupils.

General Supervision of the Health Program

In eighty-one schools a positive health program was reported. This program is directed by:

(a) the dean in 16, or 20 per cent, of the schools;

(b) the dean in coöperation with others in 31, or 38 per cent, of the schools;

(c) some other person or department in 31, or 38 per cent, of the schools.

In the twelve schools enrolling fewer than 500 pupils, only one dean assumes responsibility for the health program. In the other cases the principal, nurse, doctor, or physical education department directs the health work in the school.

In the twenty-nine schools having an enrollment of from 500 to 1,000 pupils, the following persons see that a positive health program is in effective operation:

The dean alone in 4 schools
The dean, in coöperation with others, in 8 schools
The physical education department in 8 schools
The nurse in 6 schools
The doctor and nurse in 2 schools
The home economics department in 2 schools

The nurse, teachers, dean, and physical education department in 1 school.

The doctor, nurse, dean, and physical education department in 2 schools.

A similar personnel is found in schools having an enrollment of more than 1,000 pupils. In these schools, however, the physical education, health education, and home economics departments direct the health program of the school more frequently than the nurse or doctor.

MISCELLANEOUS MARGINAL DUTIES

In addition to the specific duties already mentioned, the informal contact which the dean makes with the girls, the faculty, the parents, and visitors to the school, though less definite, is nevertheless crucial.

Ninety-five deans reported that they realize the importance of such incidental contacts as a pleasant personal greeting in the halls or on the street, a word of praise in passing by, or merely the calling of a girl by name—all these casual contacts help to establish friendly relationships between the dean and pupils.

Gaining the good will of teachers is equally important, but it will come only as a result of genuine interest in their work, sympathetic realization of their problems as co-workers in a common enterprise, and reciprocal assistance. Eighty-nine deans reported that they seek to develop an *esprit de corps* with the faculty through informal contacts, and thirty-five assist teachers and the principal more systematically in organizing social life among the faculty. Twenty-three deans, however, leave the management of the faculty social program to the teachers themselves.

Contacts with parents are made by home visits, interviews with parents in the school, and meetings of the parent-teacher association.

In eighty-one schools a certain amount of home visiting was reported. Those visits are made by:

(*a*) the dean in 33, or 41 per cent, of the schools;

(*b*) the dean and principal, teachers, nurse, or visiting teachers in 52, or 54 per cent, of the schools.

The dean plays a still more prominent part in conducting, organizing or attending meetings of the parent-teacher association. In 42, or 58 per cent, of the 73 schools reporting the existence of a parent-teacher association, the dean plays a leading rôle in it. In 29, or 40 per cent, of the schools, she coöperates with the principal, teachers, and parents in this organization. Just as experts in the field of preschool education have discovered that a large part of their work must be the education of parents, so deans also cannot fail to realize that the high school can accomplish little without assistance from parents in making the home and neighborhood environment conducive to the development of adolescents.

Eighty-seven schools entertain school visitors to some extent, and this duty devolves upon:

(a) the dean in 32, or 37 per cent, of these schools;
(b) the dean in coöperation with principal, vice-principal, and teachers in 47, or 56 per cent, of the schools.

The dean may frequently receive helpful suggestions and constructive criticism of her work from visitors from other communities. A successful dean is a real educational influence in the field, and observation of her work may be as helpful to prospective deans, and even to deans with experience, as a theoretical discussion of the position.

Duties Relating to the Office Itself

In every profession there are routine duties which must be performed before more important work can be done. Among these duties are those related to the maintenance of the office itself, such as reading and answering correspondence, organizing the work of assistants, conferring with them, answering the telephone, filing, and preparing reports from time to time.

Practically all of these deans attend to their own professional correspondence whether they have assistance or not. Approximately three-fifths organize the work of assistants who help with office work. Table XVII shows in detail the number and kind of assistants which these deans have. About half of the deans themselves at present perform miscellaneous routine office duties, but fifty-eight state positively that they think the dean should not be required to do this kind of work. Seventy-six occasionally prepare reports on their work.

As in the case of the principal, the intelligent execution of the dean's duties requires that she act on the basis of facts. The systematic recording of information concerning pupils and activities requires office equipment and organization which will save the dean's time and energy for the constructive use of such materials. Some of the devices employed by principals in the 522 schools studied by Reavis and Woellner may also be used to advantage by deans.[5]

One device widely used is the telephone. Ninety-four per cent of the principals in the study by Reavis and Woellner, and 70 per cent of deans in this study have telephones. Not one of the deans in the schools in Group I reported having a telephone in her office. It is hard to understand how a dean can maintain her contacts with parents and with the community without a telephone.

TABLE XVII

Staff of Deans of Girls

(100 Selected Deans)

	Group I	Group II	Group III	Group IV	Total (All Groups)
Assistant dean, full-time	0	0	0	2	2
Assistant dean, part-time	0	3	3	3	9
Secretary, full-time ...	0	1	1	5	7
Secretary, part-time (trained)	0	11	10	9	30
Secretary, part-time (untrained)	0	1	0	0	1
Counselors	1	6	7	13	27
Student help, full-time	0	1	0	3	4
Student help, part-time	6	22	27	20	75
Number reporting ..	12	29	31	28	100

This table is read as follows: In Groups I, II, and III, there is no school which has a full-time assistant dean. In Group IV, there are two schools which have such an officer. In the entire group of 100 schools, therefore, only two full-time assistant deans reported, etc.

Since, as Reavis and Woellner state, "the use of a typewriter means a higher standard of work and a greater amount of work," [6] it seems unfortunate that only 38 per cent of these deans have typewriters—as compared with 98 per cent of the principals in

[5] Reavis, W. C. and Woellner, Robert, "Labor-saving Devices Used in Office Administration in Secondary Schools." *The School Review*, 36:736-744, December, 1928.

[6] Ibid., p. 739.

the study previously mentioned. The dean's office, however, is better equipped in regard to files, 87 per cent of the deans reporting this essential piece of the office equipment.

As to the office itself, three-fourths of the deans reported having a private office, which, in the majority of cases, is near that of the principal and is attractively furnished. It would seem that every dean should have such necessary equipment.

Duties Relating to the Dean's Professional Growth

So rapidly is the personnel field developing that one must "keep running all the time to stay where he is." Practically all the deans in this group spend some time in keeping in touch with new developments in their vocation by attending conferences of professional people, taking courses in various phases of their work, reading recent articles, and visiting other schools. Sixty-five reported that they occasionally visited other schools; eighty, that they would like to do this more frequently. This need for knowing what other deans are doing may be met to some extent by published detailed case studies of the work of successful deans in institutions of various types. Although lacking in the vivid qualitative insight into the work which a visit gives, the published descriptions have the advantage of showing more aspects of the work, more relationships, and a more critical judgment of the performance of these duties than can be obtained in a single visit.

It is interesting in this and in other sections to note that the importance of some of the duties is generally recognized, and that there is considerable agreement concerning the duties which should belong peculiarly to the dean. It is also interesting to see how many deans at present perform duties which they do not believe germane to their task, such, for example, as supervising loitering in the halls and conduct in the cafeteria, and handling emergency cases of illness.

CHAPTER VII

RELATIONSHIP OF THE DEAN TO OTHER PEOPLE

In the two previous chapters the description given of the manifold assistance which the dean has in her work indicates clearly that the position of dean of girls is not a "one-man job." Coöperation with members of the school and of the community is essential to success in the position. The dean's relationships with the principal, teachers, her own staff, and outside agencies become crucial as the enrollment of the school increases and the dean is forced to exert her influence upon the student body more and more indirectly through the principal, teachers, pupil leaders, and outside agencies.

Relationships with the Principal

A close coöperation with the principal is characteristic of these hundred deans. In schools of all sizes practically all the deans discuss with the principal questions concerning which they wish advice. Fifty-eight reported that they consult the principal frequently about matters of all kinds, while the rest of the group confer with him only on important matters of policy. Nineteen deans said they must have his approval on all decisions concerning conduct and scholarship, while a large number—thirty-nine—seek his approval on the more important final decisions only.

The relationship between dean and principal in the smaller schools seems to differ from that in the larger schools in the degree of authority which the dean possesses. Five deans in the schools enrolling less than one thousand pupils, but only two in those with an enrollment of more than a thousand, reported that they consult the principal frequently about many minor matters. On the other hand, almost three times as many deans in larger schools said that their decisions are final and that they consult the principal only in unusual cases. Deans in large schools apparently have more individual responsibility than the majority of deans in smaller schools.

A number of deans added words of appreciation regarding their relationship with the principal: "Very cordial coöperation always"; "principal confers with me in all policies relating to the school"; "principal is very sympathetic toward the work of the dean"; "principal and I work together in formulating policies and carrying them out"; "have weekly conference with principal"; "report to principal on complex cases that he may be informed regarding them."

Relationships with Home-room Teachers, Class Advisers, and Club Sponsors

With teachers and other unofficial helpers the relation of the dean is essentially an informal one. The majority of deans reported that they maintain an informal social relationship with home-room teachers, class advisers, sponsors, and other unofficial helpers, and confer with them informally concerning their advisory work. Twenty deans reported regular and official conferences with home-room teachers and class advisers. Twenty-four said they conferred regularly and officially with club sponsors. Three deans mentioned holding a systematic training course for these assistant advisers. Thirteen deans in schools enrolling more than one thousand pupils reported frequent visits to observe the work of home-room teachers and club sponsors.

It is evident that the contacts between the dean and teachers become more regular and official as the schools increase in size, but that the deans in larger schools, while feeling the need for more systematic contact with teachers and club sponsors, recognize at the same time the value of informal conferences and social relationships with the faculty.

Relationships with Boys

In reply to the question: "Do you perform the same duties with boys as with girls?" seventy deans replied "No"; six, "Yes"; and twenty-one, "Yes, to some extent." One dean wrote—"Not officially, but in reality even more for them than for girls."

The contacts of deans of girls with boys are usually in connection with extra-curriculum activities. More than half of the deans in schools of all sizes mentioned working with boys in clubs and social activities.

Twenty-five deans spoke of classroom contacts. These contacts are more numerous in smaller than in larger schools since fewer deans teach in schools having an enrollment of over one thousand pupils.

Voluntary conferences with boys were mentioned by only five deans; interviews with boys concerning health problems by three; and interviews concerning social problems, by one.

In schools having a dean of boys, the dean of girls works indirectly with boys through him. Keeping in touch with the boys of the high school should help the dean to understand the girls better and to establish in the school a normal social life among adolescents of both sexes.

Relationships with Outside Organizations

School life of necessity involves home and community contacts. These deans both seek and give aid in a variety of neighborhood organizations. Fifty deans supplement the extra-curriculum offerings of the school by making connections with churches, Young Women's Christian Association, Campfire and Girl Scout groups.

In the treatment of some of their more serious problem cases these deans seek help from welfare organizations in thirty-two cases, from juvenile courts in seventeen cases, from public health bureaus and hospitals in sixteen cases, from associated charities in thirteen cases, from the probation officer in nine cases, and from clinics and mental hygiene associations in four cases.

In connection with the employment of pupils, seven deans have established friendly relationships with stores and business houses. Thirteen deans coöperate with the Red Cross.

Correlation between high school and elementary school at one end of the high school course and with college on the other end, is facilitated by the contacts which ten deans have with the lower school advisers and college deans.

These deans also have relationships with civic and professional groups. Thirteen belong to civic clubs, twenty-three to women's clubs including the business and professional women's clubs, and ten to the American Association of University Women.

Four deans mentioned their relationship to the press. Surely a friendly attitude on the part of reporters is most important in securing a desirable type of newspaper publicity. Through the medium of the newspaper, the parents are acquainted with the work of the dean's office.

RELATIONSHIPS WITH PARENTS

The relationships of dean with parents have already been discussed and need only be summarized here. There are three main opportunities for contacts between teachers and parents—at meetings of the parent-teacher associations, in the school when parents come to visit, and in the homes of parents. Seventy-one deans reported that they either organize, conduct, or attend meetings of the parent-teacher association. Thirteen serve on the executive committee of the association, and ten on other committees. Ninety-three deans interview parents who come to the school, and seventy visit the homes of pupils.

COMMITTEE WORK OF DEANS

If, as there is some experimental evidence to show, "two heads are better than one," the dean may, through her work on committees, contribute to group thought on certain questions, and benefit from it. From these data these questions may be answered:

On how many committees do deans serve, as chairman or as a member? On what committees do they serve?

Number of Committees. Of the ninety-three deans answering the question, all but six serve on at least one committee. One dean in a school enrolling more than a thousand girls serves on fourteen committees—on eleven as a member only and on three, as chairman. The average number of committees on which these deans serve is 4.3. The distribution is as follows:

NUMBER OF COMMITTEES		NUMBER SERVING ON COMMITTEES EITHER AS MEMBER OR CHAIRMAN
14	....	1
12	....	1
9	....	3
8	....	4
7	....	10
6	....	9
5	....	14
4	....	15
3	....	9
2	....	11
1	....	10
0	....	6

A larger number of deans serve on committees as a member rather than as chairman, the averages being 2.6 and 1.7, respectively. There is a tendency for the dean to serve on more committees in the larger than in the smaller schools. The averages for the four groups, beginning with the group of smallest schools, are: 3.3, 3.8, 4.4, 5.1. Size of school, however, does not determine whether the dean is chairman or merely a member of the committee. In the schools enrolling from 500 to 1,000 pupils the dean is more frequently the chairman than a member and as such must assume added responsibility.

Kind of Committees. In every school the dean serves on a different group of committees. One hundred and thirty-six varieties of committees are mentioned. Some of these may be essentially the same, but their names, at least, are different. They may be classified under six headings: committees relating to group activities of pupils, to group activities of teachers, to academic work, to awards and scholarships, to parents, and committees of outside organizations. In addition to these six groups, there are a few committees that could not be classified under a single heading.

COMMITTEES DEALING WITH GROUP ACTIVITIES OF PUPILS

	NUMBER OF DEANS SERVING ON COMMITTEE		
NAME OF COMMITTEE	As Member	As Chairman	Total
Social program	8	14	22
Student council	13	6	19
Committees of girls' organizations	2	8	10
Girls' Work committee of Y.W.C.A.	9	0	9
Extra-curriculum committee	4	5	9
Entertainments and plays	6	2	8
Program of school activities	5	2	7
Student dance committees	2	3	5
Senior class advisory committee	3	2	5
Student government	5	0	5
Executive committee of Girls' League	2	2	4
Committee on school paper	3	1	4
Finance	2	1	3
Preparing high school handbook	1	2	3
Point system	1	2	3
Committee on orientation of freshmen	1	2	3
Executive committee of athletic association	1	0	1
Social calendar committee	0	1	1
Report of extra-curriculum activities	1	0	1

COMMITTEES DEALING WITH GROUP ACTIVITIES OF PUPILS
(*Continued*)

	NUMBER OF DEANS SERVING ON COMMITTEE		
NAME OF COMMITTEE	As Member	As Chairman	Total
Committee for the revision of the constitution of the student government association	1	0	1
Girls' H. C. dinner dance	0	1	1
Athletic banquet	1	0	1
Athletic council	1	0	1
Program of Christmas party	0	1	1
Journalism committee	0	1	1
Senior reception	0	1	1
Junior class party—decorations committee	0	1	1
Committee having charge of the sale of candy at athletic events	0	1	1
Big Brothers and Sisters	1	0	1

COMMITTEES DEALING WITH ACADEMIC WORK OF PUPILS AND THE CURRICULUM

	NUMBER OF DEANS SERVING ON COMMITTEE		
NAME OF COMMITTEE	As Member	As Chairman	Total
Chapel program committee	17	3	20
Faculty curriculum committee	9	5	14
Health committee	6	2	8
Scholarship committee	4	2	6
Administration committee	4	1	5
Graduation	3	1	4
Committee on home-room program	1	3	4
Committees on special subjects	1	2	3
Character education committee	2	1	3
Academic program committee	2	1	3
Committee on general organization of school	2	1	3
Library committee	2	0	2
Committee for reorganizing school in accordance with the 6–3–3 plan	1	1	2
Committee on recommendations to colleges	1	0	1
Study of new marking system	1	0	1
Supervised study report	0	1	1
Honor study rooms committee	0	1	1
Committee to arrange activities for education week	1	0	1
Academic placement of pupils from other schools	0	1	1
Committee on investigation of pupils desiring to carry more or less than the normal amount of work	1	0	1

COMMITTEES DEALING WITH AWARDS AND SCHOLARSHIPS

NAME OF COMMITTEE	NUMBER OF DEANS SERVING ON COMMITTEE		
	As Member	As Chairman	Total
Awards and scholarship committee	9	7	16
Faculty committee for choosing members for the national honor society	8	1	9
Student employment	7	2	9
Awarding citizenship cup	4	1	5
Awards			
College alumnae scholarship fund	1	2	3

COMMITTEES DEALING WITH WELFARE OF TEACHERS

NAME OF COMMITTEE	NUMBER OF DEANS SERVING ON COMMITTEE		
	As Member	As Chairman	Total
Social committee of faculty	5	6	11
Professional advancement of faculty	3	1	4
Committee on teachers' room	2	1	3
Faculty general fund committee	1	2	3
Social service committee	2	0	2
Faculty committee to arrange for teachers' meetings	1	0	1
Faculty reading club	0	1	1
Faculty parties	0	1	1
Faculty purchasing committee	0	1	1
Teachers' insurance	1	0	1
Committee on the grading of teachers	0	1	1

COMMITTEES RELATING TO PARENTS

NAME OF COMMITTEE	NUMBER OF DEANS SERVING ON COMMITTEE		
	As Member	As Chairman	Total
Parent-teacher executive committee	10	3	13
Program committee of parent-teacher association ..	4	1	5
Publicity committee of parent-teacher association ..	0	2	2
Social committee of parent-teacher association	1	0	1
Parents' reading circle	1	0	1
Scholarship fund of parent-teacher association.....	1	0	1

COMMITTEES OF OUTSIDE ORGANIZATIONS

	Number of Deans Serving on Committee		
Name of Committee	As Member	As Chairman	Total
Local committee of state association of deans	3	3	6
Committee of teachers' association	1	4	5
Red Cross committee	3	1	4
Business and professional women's club	2	2	4
County social workers' club	1	2	3
Local committee for state teachers' association meeting	1	1	2
Committee of community teachers' club	1	1	2
Program committee of college entertainment club ..	0	1	1
Reception committee for women's club	1	0	1
School planning committee for district	1	0	1
Educational committee, Order of Eastern Star	1	0	1
County executive committee to plan for convention	1	0	1
Teachers' committee to elect state delegate	0	1	1
Educational committee of civic club	1	0	1
Berea Welfare Board	1	0	1
Director of A.A.U.W.	0	1	1
Loan fund committee of A.A.U.W.	0	1	1
Finance committee of A.A.U.W.	0	1	1
Executive committee of state association of deans ..	0	1	1
Survey committee for city	1	0	1
State committee for the study of outside work done by girls in high school	0	1	1
University athletic association	1	0	1
Community welfare committee of city	1	0	1
Social-civic committee of city high schools	1	0	1
Girls' work committee of church	1	0	1
State administrative women	0	1	1
Academy of Science	0	1	1
State mental hygiene association	0	1	1
Committee on status and qualifications of deans	0	1	1

MISCELLANEOUS COMMITTEES

	Number of Deans Serving on Committee		
Name of Committee	As Member	As Chairman	Total
Committee on guidance	5	6	11
Faculty cabinet	4	0	4
High school cafeteria	4	0	4
Lost and found articles	1	1	2
Buildings and grounds	2	0	2
Attendance	1	0	1

From this list, three features of the dean's committee work may be noted: (1) The great variety of committees on which deans serve; (2) the place of committee work in the direction of the social program; and (3) the committees on which deans serve most frequently.

The variety of committees shows the place of the dean in policy making and the possibilities of many contacts with pupils, teachers, parents, and professional people outside of the school. Some of the committees here listed may suggest to deans or principals means of saving time by discussing certain school problems in groups rather than in individual conferences. In directing the social program, these deans frequently gain assistance from teachers and pupils in group conferences.

The specific committees on which deans serve most frequently are those relating to the social program, the student council, the chapel program, the curriculum, awards and scholarships, the social life of the faculty, the parent-teacher association, and state and national associations of deans.

CHAPTER VIII

CASE STUDY OF THE WORK OF DEAN OF GIRLS IN ONE HIGH SCHOOL

The analysis of duties in the previous chapter, useful as it is for intensive study of specific phases of the dean's work, fails to give a unified picture of the dean in action. A case study of one institution, including a typical detailed daily schedule, will add vividness to the statistical treatment of the work of a hundred selected deans.

The case study describes a specific situation, and shows the dean at work in this situation and her relationship to the pupils, principal, teachers, outside agencies, and other officers of the school. It is the nearest approach to a visit to the institution—a visit of a number of days' duration during which the observation of the visitor is supplemented by explanations and critical comments of the dean herself.

The school chosen for the case study is one in which the advisory work has received the sincere and unsolicited commendation of superintendent, principal, and teachers.

DESCRIPTION OF THE SITUATION

Setting. The high school used for this study is one of four senior high schools in a mid-western city of 160,000 population. Two of these four schools are combination junior and senior high schools. There are, in addition, six separate junior high schools in the system. Each junior and each senior high school in the city has on its administrative staff a dean of girls and, with the exception of two small junior high schools, a vice-principal and dean of boys as well.

Size of Institution. The school has an enrollment of 1,458 pupils —675 boys and 763 girls. There is a faculty of 49 teachers in addition to the chairmen of departments. The administrative force includes the principal, vice-principal and dean of boys, dean of girls, registrar, and a full-time trained secretary.

Student Body. Approximately 98 per cent of the student population were born in America. About 7 per cent are children of Jewish parents, 5 per cent are of negro birth, and a very small percentage of the remainder are of foreign parentage from various European countries.

The school serves a community made up of the substantial middle class in which there is neither great wealth nor extreme poverty. Most of the parents own their own homes and are engaged in the trades, both skilled and unskilled, in mercantile or in clerical work. Approximately 40 per cent of the girls and 65 per cent of the boys earn a part or all of their high school expenses. All but a very small number of girls live in their own homes. This small number (usually about 15 or 20 girls) come to the city for its school advantages. These girls live in the homes of relatives or give a few hours' service in private homes in order to earn their living expenses.

Very few of the parents have had a college education, but they are eager to secure its benefits for their boys and girls. Approximately 40 per cent of the pupils continue their education in higher institutions, the majority attending local and state colleges and universities. A few attend the business colleges in the city after graduation. Of those going to work at once, a small percentage enroll in the evening classes provided by the public school system.

The Staff. The dean has neither trained assistant nor secretary, but the principal's secretary is available when trained clerical assistance is necessary.

A varying number of student assistants help with office routine. The dean feels that there is a large educational value for the girls in such work and that she has thus an opportunity also to become intimately acquainted with a larger number of girls. The training of pupils, of course, takes time, but from the standpoint of office practice the time is spent to better advantage than if the dean were to do the actual routine work herself, and from an educational point of view may well be a part of her program for girls.

In addition to the pupil assistants, the dean's staff consists of what may be termed the "social faculty." In this group are included the thirty-five home-room advisers, the 14 club advisers, the advisers of the senior class (the only class in the city high schools which is organized), the adviser of various student council activities over some of which the dean has general supervision, and the literary adviser of school publications.

The vice-principal and dean of boys coöperates with the dean of girls in carrying out the plans of the social program, but his time is largely consumed with the administrative duties of a vice-principal.

The school nurse is in reality an assistant to the dean in the scope of her work and in her method of handling problems.

Chart I presents the relation of the dean to the organization as a whole.

Duties

Personal Advisement of Pupils

Orientation and Advisement of New Pupils. The program of orientation and advisement of new pupils consists in acquainting each entering pupil and his parents with the program of studies, with the program of student activities, and with the traditions and regulations of the school; in providing each home-room adviser with all of the information obtainable about each advisee; in making it possible for the home-room adviser to capitalize this information in the orientation and guidance work; and in helping the pupil to feel at home in the new environment as quickly as possible.

The dean's part in this program is that of working with the dean of boys in coördinating and supervising its various phases. The two deans visit the junior high schools to meet prospective pupils in group conferences and, where necessary for a better general understanding of the offerings of the new school, individual conferences. They assign these pupils to home-room advisers in sufficient time for each adviser to become acquainted with the guidance work of the junior high school deans, before he meets his advisees. They assist the home-room advisers in making adjustments to care for individual needs and in giving guidance in special cases. With the home-room advisers they plan ways by which home-room officers and student committees can assist in the orientation to the new social and physical environment.

Educational and Vocational Guidance. The chief function of the home-room is guidance. The home-room advisers, with the dean of girls as an advisory member of the group, have made an intensive study of the objectives and work of the home-room in terms of this function. The dean uses this syllabus as a basis for the supervision of the home-room guidance work. An educational guidance bulletin which explains the offering and requirements of all the city high schools, together with the requirements of colleges and universities most frequently attended by graduates of the city high school, supplements the syllabus.

The home-room adviser is responsible for the continuous educational and vocational guidance of an advisee from the time he enters until he leaves high school, though the deans consult with him and often work directly with cases referred to them by the adviser.

Improvement in Scholarship. The dean's relation to the academic work of the girls is advisory rather than administrative. She receives reports of each girl's academic standing each marking period and interviews girls who are falling behind in their work in order to give constructive aid for improvement. She interviews parents, classroom teachers, and home-room advisers, if necessary, in order to understand the situation. She also interviews girls who are apparently not working up to the level of their ability. With the home-room adviser and, if necessary, the principal, she devises such means for improvement of unsatisfactory work as the situation demands.

The dean is an ex officio member of a faculty student scholarship committee which studies ways and means of raising scholarship. Each department chairman and classroom teacher is responsible for teaching "how to study" methods in his particular subject. The dean assists these people by leading discussions on study habits with groups of new pupils and by aiding faculty and student committees in arranging home-room discussions on such topics as time budgeting and the value of achievement.

Health. The department of health which includes a health supervisor, a nurse, a physician for boys and one for girls, physical education teachers for boys and for girls, and a swimming instructor is primarily responsible for the health of the girls. Various clinics in the community are also available for school use. The dean keeps in close touch with the health situation regarding individual girls and often refers health problem cases which she has discovered to the department. Emergency cases of illness in the absence of the nurse are the only ones handled by the dean's office. The nurse and the social worker from the attendance department do follow-up work, and keep the dean informed of progress in that work. There is the closest coöperation between the dean's office and the health office.

A faculty and student health committee of which the dean is an ex-officio member is doing valuable work in detecting shortages in the health situation and in launching health projects.

Attendance. The dean interviews only exceptional cases of absence or tardiness. The home-room adviser readmits on her own authority all absentees to classes except in cases of illness, when she requires the approval of the nurse. All absentees are reported to the dean's office early in the day. A pupil trained for the work makes telephone calls to the home (about 85 per cent of the homes have telephones) except in special cases. These the dean reports to a social case worker of the attendance department. The reports from telephone calls and from the social case worker are forwarded to the home-room adviser.

The vice-principal and dean of boys handles, with the aid of a teacher at a "tardy desk," all cases of tardiness. Only those indicating maladjustment of girls are sent to the dean of girls.

Employment. The dean keeps a file of all girls wishing part-time employment as well as a file of information concerning all people who have registered a desire for part-time help. A social case worker from the attendance department investigates homes which are asking for the services of the girls, except in those cases in which the dean is acquainted with the home situation. The dean also keeps in touch with personnel managers of factories, insurance companies, department stores, and the telephone company. The chairman of the commercial department aids the dean by investigating opportunities for girls who need to earn money when such placement involves commercial training.

Scholarships and Loans. The dean makes recommendations to the Scholarship Committee of the city parent-teacher council when help is needed to keep the girl in school if the case is deemed a worthy one. The head of the attendance department, who is chairman of this committee, coöperates with the dean in making the investigations and often in locating the cases. The local parent-teacher association also coöperates with the dean in helping to find work to keep girls in school and in providing clothing, school supplies, or in meeting other needs.

Personal Social Problems. The dean seeks to have the atmosphere of her office such that girls will come voluntarily to discuss personal social problems. Reference to the dean's files show that about 90 per cent of interviews of this type are voluntary. The dean assists home-room advisers in the work that they are doing along this line whenever her assistance is solicited.

Discover and Follow-up Cases of Maladjustment. The dean is assisted by practically every agency in school and community in the discovery of maladjustment cases. The fine coöperation of home-room advisers, classroom teachers, members of parent-teacher association, social workers and head of the attendance department, club advisers, health department, other members of the administrative group, and even students themselves make it possible to discover cases of maladjustment—such as superior girls doing average or inferior work, dull girls having trouble in doing high school work, unsocial girls, over-social girls, girls below par in health, girls who are problem cases because of social maladjustment outside of school. Every agency of the school and community is likewise at the command of the dean in the follow-up work with these cases.

Discipline. The dean of girls is not considered a disciplinary officer in academic matters. The principal feels that the dean can not accomplish her best work by such an assignment of duties. Home-room advisers and, in exceptional cases, the principal, care for situations in which disciplinary measures are required.

Group Activities

Supervision of Social Curriculum

The supervision of the social curriculum of the school takes a large share of the dean's time. In this phase of her work she has contacts with boys as well as girls.

Student Council and Home-Room. Principal, vice-principal dean of girls, and a member of the faculty, officially appointed, work directly with the student government association which is composed of the presidents, vice-presidents, and secretaries of the thirty-five home-rooms. Only the presidents, however, are voting members.

The dean of girls attends the weekly meetings of the student council. She assists in the general advisory work and is responsible for the supervision of certain of its activities. She is the adviser for the joint student council and faculty committees on citizenship which plan the course of study for the home-room discussion program. In this connection she meets each week the thirty-five home-room vice-presidents who are, by virtue of their office, home-room discussion leaders, and works out with them the details of the plans and outlines proposed by the student-faculty committee.

The dean is the adviser for the Committee on School Social Life, working with them directly as they develop their objectives and as they outline their social program for carrying out these objectives. She has indirect supervision of the detailed program which they evolve under the direct guidance of faculty advisers. She is a guest of the social affairs which include receptions to new students, teas, evening parties, and dances, supper parties, matinee dances, Friday afternoon social hours, a series of Christmas parties, an all-school honor party, and the annual frolic.

The dean also works as an advisory member with the joint student-faculty Activities Committee. This committee seeks to find out what new activities are needed to supplement those in school and community. It recommends to the student council, after consideration, requests for new organizations, keeps in the dean's office up-to-date files of club constitutions and membership, plans home-room discussions so as to acquaint all pupils with the school's activity program, informs parents through the parent-teacher association of the objectives and scope of this program, attempts to draw in the unsocial and to keep a nice balance of extra-curriculum work in which pupils may be engaged. This committee is assisted in its work by a representative in each home-room.

The dean advises the Booster Committee which, as its name indicates, aids in the promotion of school projects. It plans assemblies for advertising dramatics and rallies for athletic games. It boosts the parent-teacher association membership campaign and stands behind the Public Welfare drive. It, too, has a representative in each home-room for encouraging and advertising any project launched in the school.

The dean is a member of scholarship, award and health committees. The work of these committees is carried out by both students and faculty, meeting as separate and as joint bodies.

The Club Program. The dean supervises the club program of the school. The club advisers, with the dean as an advisory member of the group, have studied intensively the purposes and underlying philosophy of a club program and have assembled their findings in a "Syllabus for Clubs." This syllabus gives a statement of regulations and of objectives, a suggested scheme of organization, suggested plans and procedures for an individual club, a model constitution, instructions for club treasurers, sample budgets, suggested induction ceremonies, and statements of belief as to value of insignia, ceremonial, and creeds as well as criteria for evaluating the work of the club. This syllabus, which has been discussed and accepted by the faculty, is used as the basis for supervision. The dean receives copies of semester programs and budgets, attends club meetings occasionally, confers with club advisers and committees, and as a guest, attends many social affairs of the various clubs.

The Social Calendar. The dean has charge of the social calendar which is made at the beginning of each semester when each organization files a statement as to the type of affair planned and the time desired. Each home-room is provided with a copy of the calendar and receives notices of any addendum. More detailed forms are filed in the dean's office at least a week before a particular affair is held.

The Senior Class. The dean spends much time as the adviser of the senior class. She is assisted in the work by a number of faculty sponsors who advise the seniors in planning a varied and interesting social program which includes the activities of commencement week, and in organizing and carrying out the activities incidental to graduation. The dean of girls, vice-principal, and principal have individual interviews with seniors for giving educational and vocational advice when such advice is desired. The dean interviews all seniors falling behind in their work and plans with them ways of bringing their work up to standard.

Alumni. The dean advises the committee planning the annual alumni reception. A permanent class secretary for each out-going class and a faculty adviser, officially appointed, keep in touch with alumni although there is no formal organization.

Control of Physical Environment

The dean acts in an incidental advisory capacity only, in the control of the physical environment. Student committees with faculty advisers supervise conduct in the lunchroom and corridors; the health department supervises first-aid equipment; the student-faculty health committee, with the aid of the matron, supervises rest rooms and sanitary conditions in the building and refers such matters to the proper authorities.

Control of Intellectual Environment

Principal, vice-principal, and dean meet in conference each Saturday morning for discussion concerning curriculum, pupils' programs, methods of instruction, discipline, and future administrative policies. The dean confers by appointment at the middle of each six weeks' marking period with all classroom teachers concerning girls who are falling behind in their work. She consults with the home-room adviser in the matter of change in study and extra-curriculum programs of the girls. She checks each girl's educational guidance sheet once during the semester.

The dean attends faculty meetings which are often devoted to a discussion of various phases of the social curriculum in its relation to the academic curriculum, with the dean or a member of the social faculty leading the discussion. She attends assemblies and often advises assembly committees such as those planning the student council induction assembly with its formal ritual, the National Honor Society induction service, as well as assemblies planned by the Booster Committee.

Marginal Duties

The dean seeks as many ways as possible for informal contacts with girls and faculty. Much of the informal contact with faculty comes from the fine congeniality of this faculty which manifests itself in many informal social affairs planned by various members of the group.

The dean makes few home visits, but has many formal and informal contacts with parents in her office. With the principal and dean of boys she entertains school visitors and represents the girls as occasion requires.

A parent-teacher association of one thousand members which is so organized that a "home-room mother" for each home-room is responsible for interesting her small group of mothers in attendance and in participation in the activities of the larger group reflects the fine spirit of coöperation, understanding, and backing which the school receives from its community. The dean has no formal responsibility for its program or meetings. She attends its meetings and coöperates in every way possible in promoting its activities.

Committees. The dean is a member of the Faculty Council which decides important school policies, a member of the Honors Award Committee, an ex officio member of faculty committees on scholarship, activities, and citizenship. She is a member of the Committee on Recreational Standards of the City Council of Parent-Teacher Associations.

Research. Information about individual girls is accumulated by both the dean and the registrar. The dean collects and studies data concerning graduates of the school. Reports of club activities and school organizations furnish material for statistical study. A complete survey of the extra-curriculum situation is made every two years and the findings used as material on which to base an improved and adequate social program.

Teaching. The dean teaches five hours a week—a class in social science.

Office Hours and Duties. The dean's office hours are from eight to five o'clock on school days and from eight to one o'clock on Saturdays with the exception of one hour for daily classroom teaching. At least two hours each Saturday morning are reserved for conference with principal and vice-principal. Committee meetings usually average two hours a day and a large proportion of the remaining time is consumed in conferences with pupils, classroom teachers, home-room and club advisers and officers, and parents.

The dean dictates correspondence and special bulletins to a secretary whom the principal shares with her. Girls from advanced classes in office practice give such clerical assistance as filing, keeping card files up to date, and typing. Material for the social program is mimeographed in the commercial department and in the school office. Pupil assistants telephone homes of absentees, except in special cases, answer the telephone, make appointments for the dean, and show courtesies to visitors.

DAILY SCHEDULE

A more concrete picture of the dean's duties may be obtained by considering the schedule of an actual day. The following record kept by the dean is as typical of her daily duties as a single day's schedule can be.

TYPICAL DAILY SCHEDULE

7:45– 8:00 Conference with chairman of Booster Committee.

8:00– 8:10 Conference with pupil who is giving clerical assistance in office.

8:10– 8:15 Conference by telephone with mother concerning girl who wants to stop school.

8:15– 8:20 Conference with girl who is worried about poor marks received on report card.

8:20–8:22 Conference with chairman of the social committee of the French Club concerning French Club tea.

8:22– 8:25 Conference by telephone with housewife who wishes a girl for part-time work.

8:25– 8:30 Conference by telephone with social case worker.

8:30– 8:40 Conference with adviser of Girls' Athletic Association concerning new point system of awards.

8:40– 8:50 Conference with principal concerning letters to be sent to prospective junior high school patrons.

8:50– 9:10 Conference with girl who is falling very low in her work.

9:10– 9:25 Conference with representative from juvenile home concerning problem case.

9:25– 9:28 Telephone conversation concerning qualifications of girl who is applying for job in telephone office.

9:28– 9:35 Read and answered mail.

9:35– 9:40 Telephone conversation with dean of girls in another high school concerning program of state dean's association.

9:40– 9:50 Conference with president of senior class.

9:50–10:00 Conference with girl who is overworking.

10:00–10:35 Conference with girl who is having home troubles.

10:35–11:07 Taught class.

11:07–11:12 Conference with reporter for school paper.

11:22–11:42 Visited two home-rooms.

11:42–11:53 Conference with home-room adviser on disciplinary case.

11:53–12:00 Looked over lists of absentees, called attendance department, conferred with girl who telephones homes of absentees.

12:00–12:10 Interview with home-room adviser concerning social guidance problem.

12:10–12:30 Lunch.

12:30– 1:00 Conference with girl who wants to stop school to go to work.

1:00– 1:10 Conference with sponsor of National Honor Society.

1:10– 1:15 Telephone conference with president of parents teachers association concerning next week's meeting.

1:15– 1:30 Visited with several teachers in rest room.

1:30– 1:53 Made plans for meeting with home-room vice-presidents.

1:53– 2:33 Attended student council meeting.

2:33– 3:15 Met with thirty-five home-room vice-presidents to consider home room discussion for following week.

3:15– 3:45 Met with faculty Activities Committee.

3:45– 4:15 Conference with mother and daughter—misunderstanding between home and school.

4:15– 4:30 Visited in social rooms with group of girls and boys preparing decorations for Friday night party.

4:30– 4:40 Discussed several senior records with registrar.

4:45– 6:30 Girls' Athletic Association picnic.

The dean kept a similar record for a week. An idea of the amount of time devoted to various phases of the work may be obtained from a study of the schedule of a typical week which follows.

SUMMARY OF SCHEDULE OF A TYPICAL WEEK

AVERAGE NUMBER
OF MINUTES PER DAY

Personal Advisement of Students

1. Interviewing students on personal problems
   a. Study problems 15.2
   b. Health problems 6.0
   c. Financial difficulties 3.0
   d. Employment opportunities 7.2
   e. Educational guidance, including advice concerning academic program, choice of college, etc. 8.0
   f. Miscellaneous personal problems 44.4
2. Interviewing students concerning
   a. Absence and tardiness 10.0
   b. Misconduct 6.3
3. Interviewing teachers and home-room advisers concerning personal problems of students, and disciplinary policies 29.6
4. Investigating opportunities for employment of students 8.4
5. Administering student loans and scholarships 2.5

   Total 140.6

Group Activities of Students

6. Directing social life and extra class room activities
   a. Attending meetings, social events, including chaperoning 65.0
   b. Assisting student committees in planning social events 10.2
   c. Having charge of social calendar 1.4
   d. Conferring with officers and committees of student organizations 17.2
   e. Conferring with sponsors of student organizations and social events 25.5
   f. Personally supervising student government 20.0
7. Addressing groups of students 3.2
8. Securing speakers to address students 1.0
9. Working with senior officers and committees 10.0
10. Entertaining school visitors 8.0
11. Arranging opportunities for students to engage in social service .. 2.0

   Total 163.5

Control of the Physical Environment

12. Maintaining a positive health program 15.3
13. Supervising girls living away from home 3.0
14. Conferring with principal and other officers of the school concerning school environment 2.0

   Total 20.3

Control of the Intellectual Environment

15. Teaching 35.4
16. Attending faculty meetings 12.0
17. Attending assembly 9.0
18. Conferring with principal or teachers concerning absence, academic work or individual pupils and courses of study, and special programs 19.0

Total 75.4

Personal Development of the Dean Herself

19. Studying, including reading professional material, preparing for teaching classes, attending lectures and conferences 67.8

Management of the Dean's Office

20. Reading and answering correspondence 12.5
21. Miscellaneous office duties including answering the telephone .. 20.0
22. Keeping records and writing reports 5.0
23. Looking over records of pupils, collecting data concerning individual pupils 7.8
24. Supervising student assistants 15.0

Total 60.3

Miscellaneous Marginal Duties

25. Informal contact with students 12.0
26. Informal contact with teachers, and other professional associates 20.0
27. Interviewing parents, including telephone calls with parents 15.0
28. Speaking to local organizations 6.0
29. Committee meetings 10.0
30. Conference with principal and other officers concerning miscellaneous matters 23.8

Total 86.8
Total average time spent daily in the dean's work 614.7

Conclusion

The broad vision of the superintendent and his unfailing confidence in the value of a dean of girls to a school, the inspiring leadership together with the enthusiasm and supervision of the principal, the hearty coöperation of the faculty in both academic and social phases of the work, the good will and fine constructive attitude of the parents and the community, and finally the spirit of good fellowship of girls and boys all combine to challenge the dean to her best and make possible the joys of accomplishment.

CHAPTER IX

PROFESSIONAL SATISFACTIONS AND PROBLEMS OF THE POSITION OF DEAN OF GIRLS

Women interested in preparing for the vocation of dean of girls wish to know not only the possible openings in the field, the vocational route by which deans have reached the position, the salary which may be expected, the experience and training required, and the duties which deans perform, but also they wish to know the satisfactions and problems of the position.

Some of the rewards and problems of personnel work may be surmised from the description of the duties given in previous chapters, but the deans' own statements regarding the satisfactions they feel in their work and the main problems which they have encountered is of considerable interest.

Professional Satisfactions To the question: "What do you think are the main professional satisfactions of the position of dean of girls?" nine deans made no reply. Nineteen deans frankly stated their satisfaction in the prestige which is attached to the position. One mentioned the increase in salary—a consideration not to be ignored.

The majority of these deans emphasized the opportunities for service which the position affords. This aspect of the work was stated in a number of ways: "Opportunity to direct youth"; "opportunity for vocational guidance"; "helping youth to develop a philosophy of life"; "contribution to character education."

Forty-one deans mentioned the pleasure in working with young people: "Seeing girls grow"; "friendship with girls"; "association with youth"; "opportunity to discuss vital matters with girls"; "satisfaction in seeing pupils happy and doing worthwhile things"; "challenge of problem girls"; "enjoyment in working with people"; "straightening out difficulties of individual girls."

A smaller number of deans—twenty—reported satisfaction in

97

the executive aspects of the work, its stimulating, challenging quality, the thrill of "pioneering in a new field," the large responsibilities of the position, the opportunity to grow with the work, the lack of monotony, the contacts with other professional people, and the tangible accomplishment of aims.

These are the satisfactions which we should expect to find in the position—pleasure in associating with adolescent boys and girls; satisfaction in having a chance to help each pupil develop to the extent of his or her capacity; and opportunity for the dean herself to grow and advance professionally in a type of work congenial to her.

Problems of the Position. One of the ways in which deans can contribute to the professional advancement of the dean's position is by carefully noting problems which need scientific study. Many of the problems suggested by these deans are suitable subjects for research. Others call attention to necessary administrative changes. Forty-seven deans mentioned their own lack of understanding of the position as well as the lack of understanding on the part of the family, the administration, and the public. One spoke of the feeling that the dean's office was a disciplinary one.

This investigation should be helpful in solving the group of problems relating to the definition of the dean's work.

Chapters V and VI of this report and the table in Appendix C, which describe in detail the duties which a hundred selected deans of girls perform, should be especially valuable for this purpose. Any dean who is vague about the scope of her work might be helped by studying each of these duties in reference to her own situation. Principals, teachers, and parents ought also to gain a better understanding of the dean's work by reading those chapters.

A second type of problem which might be included under the first is that of organization of the dean's work. Eleven deans mentioned lack of time; two, lack of organization; one, multiplicity of duties; five, the indefinite and unbounded scope of the work; nine, multiplicity of baffling detail; ten, lack of assistants; three, number of large undertakings; two, length of hours and endless demands; three, too much teaching; one, constant interruption in her work; five, difficulty in keeping one's perspective; two, continual demand for discriminating judgment; and one, lack of time for follow-up of cases.

A third type of problem is that of securing coöperation. Eight deans mentioned the problem of securing the coöperation of the faculty; two, jealousy; one, "overcoming the feeling on the part of some that the work is not important."

A fourth problem is that of securing adequate preparation for the work. Two spoke of lack of organized courses for deans; two, lack of training and experience; one, lack of techniques; one, lack of specific knowledge.

A fifth group of problems relate to difficulties inherent in the work. Three deans mentioned lack of tangible results; two, the difficulty of reaching individuals at the time when help is most needed; seven, the difficulty of making personal contacts with such a large number of pupils; eight, the difficulty of helping serious problem cases; two, the tendency to advise too freely.

Lack of equipment was referred to by four deans; inadequate salary, by seven; lack of recognition on the part of the public, by seven; the difficulty of a position as "buffer between principal and teachers," by ten.

The frequency with which these problems are mentioned is not necessarily a true indication of their importance. Some problems which are mentioned only once are worthy of intensive study. Some of the main problems which should be investigated in the near future are the following:

1. How may the dean's work in a particular institution be surveyed in order to determine which of the complete list of personnel duties should be performed in her school, and which should be performed by the dean alone or in coöperation with others, and how many assistants of different kinds the dean should have in a school of a given size and type.

2. What is the most effective way of performing each of the specific duties? The solution of this problem requires a job analysis of each phase of the dean's work.

3. What methods have successful deans used in securing the coöperation of teachers and special officers of the school, of advisers in elementary schools and colleges, and of outside agencies?

4. To what extent should a professional course include laboratory and field work as well as theory?

5. Which specific techniques are needed in the dean's work? How may these techniques best be acquired?

6. What specific knowledge is needed in performing each of the major duties? Which phases of this knowledge may be secured in courses, and which "on the job"?

7. How may cases of maladjustment be detected in their early stages? What are the best methods of handling particular types of cases of maladjustment? Who are the persons best qualified to do this work?

8. What equipment should be furnished the dean in order to save her time and energy?

9. What quantitative and qualitative measures may the dean use to gauge and to demonstrate the success of her work?

10. How may the importance of the dean's work be more convincingly demonstrated to principals, faculty, and the general public?

CHAPTER X

EVALUATION OF THE WORK OF THE DEAN OF GIRLS

An evaluation of a person's work may be made by the person himself, by other people in intimate association with him, and, on a theoretical basis, by a specialist who surveys the work.

This chapter will include the deans' own estimate of the various phases of their work in which they have accomplished most, and those in which they have accomplished least; the favorable and unfavorable comments on their work which have come to their attention; and a discussion of the status and function of these hundred selected deans from the standpoint of educational theory.

THE DEANS' OWN EVALUATION OF THEIR WORK

In answer to the question, "In which phases of your work do you think you have accomplished most?" deans in schools of all sizes mention results which they have achieved in the personal advisement of students and in the supervision of the social program.

Through personal interviews and other contacts, some of these deans feel they have improved the morale of the school, won the confidence of the girls, helped them "to think through problems" and in general to adjust better to school life.

Approximately one-fourth of the hundred deans spoke of their success in enlarging, readjusting, or directing the social program. Several mentioned, specifically, effective work in the Girls' League, and other girls' organizations. The point system, group discussions on social responsibility, the creating of "an atmosphere conducive to good manners and desirable social experience," the making of school social affairs more simple, and the interesting of the principal and faculty in the social program were other phases of school life to which the deans felt that they had made a contribution.

Success in educational guidance and the orientation of freshmen was mentioned occasionally; success in vocational guidance, rarely. Decreased absence and improved scholarship were offered as objective evidence of accomplishment.

Two deans in schools enrolling from 500 to 1,000 girls spoke with pride of their part in the health program. Contacts with parents and community, and faculty coöperation were mentioned by a few deans in the schools enrolling more than 500 pupils. One dean claimed that she had "sold" the office to the principal, and another spoke of success in making the dean's position "a dignified and respected one."

In answer to the question: "In which phases of your work do you think you have accomplished least?" thirteen deans replied, "A positive health program"; and thirteen others, "Vocational guidance."

Approximately one-fourth of the deans spoke of their lack of success in directing the social program. Four felt they had accomplished least with the Girls' League; ten, in general social organizations; six, in the supervision of clubs; three, in providing an adequate social life; two, in making extra-curriculum activities function for all girls; two, in interesting the faculty in club activities; and one, in securing desirable behavior in dance halls.

Thirty-one deans recognized their lack of success in various aspects of personal advisement; eight in follow-up work; seven in case work; three in personal interviews; five in problem cases; three in the orientation of freshmen; four in personal contacts in general; and one in home adjustments. Ten deans said that they had accomplished least in educational guidance and the improvement of scholarship.

Four deans mention lack of success in various aspects of the organization of their office such as "freeing myself from detail"; "letting little things interfere with big things"; and "getting secretarial help." In contrast to one who felt that she had won the principal to an appreciation of her work, six deans felt they had accomplished least in "selling" their work to the principal and faculty, and in gaining desirable publicity.

In order properly to evaluate the comments of the deans themselves on their own work, it would be necessary to study each individual dean in connection with the entire set-up of her work, and the extent to which she has authority and opportunity to work toward chosen objectives. The personal characteristics and training of the dean should also be considered. Are the ten deans who feel that they have accomplished least in educational guidance and in the improvement of scholarship so tied by clerical detail that they have little time for such constructive work, or is it because the dean herself has no vision of that phase of activity as a part of her task? Is the lack of success in the various aspects of personal advisement reported by thirty-one deans due to very high standards as to what success is, to a lack of knowledge of adolescent psychology, or to personal inability to reach boys and girls? It is probable that the comments yield no real facts except in the sense that an idea is a fact with which to reckon. As isolated statements they mean little except as they have been the result of self-evaluation.

In reading these comments, however, one is impressed not only by the constructive nature of work which deans are trying to accomplish, but also by the lack of definite objective measurement of results. Many results of the dean's work are to be sure, intangible, but many others, such as reduction of absences, improvement in scholarship, number of pupils who come to the dean voluntarily for guidance in individual or group activities, and number of contacts with parents and outside agencies lend themselves to quantitative measurement.

In order to obtain the most accurate knowledge of the results of her work, the dean should combine these quantitative indications of effective work with the impressions which she gets from the comments and attitude of pupils, principal, faculty, and parents.

Other Peoples' Evaluation of the Dean's Work

In evaluating the comments, favorable and unfavorable, which are made concerning the dean's work, one must remember that the dean herself has recorded what may be only chance remarks of some individuals, people who may in no way represent a common opinion of the strength or weakness of the dean's work Her work in connection with health may be highly approved by the director of physical education, or may arouse her jealousy and unfavorable remark. Neither expressed opinion would be a true judgment of the worth of her work. Words of praise or blame which come back to the dean often assume unwarranted importance. Like the deans' opinions of their own work, they mean little except in connection with a total situation, and are interesting only as they may indicate pitfalls into which some people, at least, think that deans may fall.

Favorable Comments. At least seventy different answers were given to the question: "Which specific parts of your work have been, as far as you know, commented on especially favorably by students or faculty?" Although these comments come to us through the medium of the dean's interpretation, they are interesting as indications of the attitude of the faculty as well as of the accomplishments of the dean.

The largest number of commendations refer to the dean's direction of group activities of pupils. The following specific phases of this work were mentioned:

Duty	Frequency
Organization and direction of the social program and extra-curriculum activities	28
Supervision of the Girls' League	18
Supervision of the student government	5
Health program	3
Vocational conference	3
Social service activities	3
Senior class activities	3
Athletic program	1
Home-room program	1
Organization of girls into clubs	1
Big Sister plan	1
Fairer distribution of the extra-curriculum duties of teachers	1
Enlarged social life	1
Social program for teachers	1
Total	70

The dean's work with individuals was approved as frequently as their work with groups. The following specific phases of this work were mentioned:

Duty	Frequency
Personal advisement in general	22
Work with problem cases	10
Educational guidance	9
Administration of discipline	9
Orientation of entering pupils	6
Contacts with the homes	4

Helping failing pupils 3
Vocational guidance and placement 3
Care of sick girls 2
Adjustment of girls of low I.Q. 1
Personality ratings of pupils 1

Total 70

It is natural that the two phases of the work. to which the largest number of these deans devote the major portion of their time are those which frequently receive favorable comments.

Some less tangible results of the deans' work were also spoken of with approval:

RESULTS OF THE DEAN'S WORK	FREQUENCY
Raising the morale of the school	14
Gaining the confidence of the girls	12
Coöperation with the faculty and nurse	11
Improvement in scholarship of pupils	7
Improvement in dress and appearance of girls	3
Increased initiative on the part of the girls	2
Keeping girls in school	2
Better attendance—less truancy	2
Good fellowship existing in school	1
Improvement in manners	1
Improvement in order of study hall	1
Friendship with girls leaving school	1
Enriched curriculum	1
Organization of the library	1

Total 59

The following favorable comments were made concerning the personal qualities of the deans:

	FREQUENCY
Friendliness and helpfulness	4
Best in handling problems	4
"Fair play" of dean	3
Ability to speak in assembly	2
Ability to "iron out" trouble	2
Ability to organize her work	2
Ability to appeal to girls	1
Ability to plan and carry out school policies	1
Enthusiasm	1
Professional spirit	1
"Principal and superintendent consider the dean a right arm"	1

Total 22

The favorable opinions of faculty and pupils regarding the dean's work indicate the personnel duties which attract the attention of the faculty, as well as those which are performed by the dean in an exceptionally effective way. It may be true that these deans are successful in types of work which have not been recognized by faculty or pupils, or have not been mentioned to her.

Unfavorable Comments. As might be expected, adverse criticism of the dean's work does not reach her as frequently as praise. Twenty-one deans did not answer this question; fourteen reported no unfavorable comments; and fourteen others remarked that "none were reported to them" or that they were "not likely to hear them." Nevertheless the unfavorable comments reported by deans, though not so numerous as the favorable opinions, are very enlightening. They suggest types of activity on the dean's part which may cause the antagonism of certain members of the faculty.

Lack of coöperation with certain teachers was reported five times. Two teachers mentioned resentment on the part of the faculty; one spoke of the "jealousy of some teachers who think I am an interloper"; another reported the criticism that she "takes too much authority for her age."

The dean's relation to discipline received eight unfavorable comments: "Too sympathetic with pupils"; "dean too severe to some students"; "some of the faculty wish the dean to be a disciplinarian of the old type"; "dean too lenient in punishing."

The dean's direction of the social program was criticized from many angles: "Too meticulous supervision of dances"; "faculty resent suggestions regarding the social program"; "social affairs are too elaborate"; "dean does not attend enough club meetings"; "too little supervision of some activities"; "new sponsors have difficulty in understanding the red tape"; "faculty think dean should chaperone all parties." These and similar opinions regarding the dean's supervision of extra-curriculum activities were reported by ten deans.

Six criticisms related to the organization of the dean's office. Among the comments made were: "Too great centralization"; "vagueness of dean's duties"; "too much red tape"; "difficult to see dean"; "faculty wonder what dean does to keep busy"; "too much time given to one individual."

The following unfavorable comments regarding personal characteristics of the dean were frankly reported: "Individual pupils feel dean's office is a place to avoid"; "dean has old-fashioned ideas about some things"; "dean is impatient with assistants." Each of these statements was made once.

The remaining miscellaneous criticisms were of the dean's relation to the home-room program; her censorship of school publications; her neglect of a particular grade; the personality rating sheets she wished the faculty to fill out; and her insistence on educational guidance.

It would be impossible to generalize from these comments regarding possibilities of success or failure which may confront the dean, since they often refer to the individual personal limitations of the dean or her co-workers, or to conflicting ideas concerning the nature of the dean's work. Such a comment as "too sympathetic with pupils" might be rooted in either condition or both. Some do, however, point out dangers which might easily grow out of excellence if it were carried to an extreme. Good organization might grow into "too much red tape" or high social standards lead to "too meticulous supervision of dances."

THEORETICAL EVALUATION AND DISCUSSION OF THE POSITION OF DEAN OF GIRLS

Do these hundred deans represent the ideal practice? How may their status be improved? Which phases of their work seem most valuable from a theoretical standpoint?

Prevalence of the Position. In recent state studies referred to in Table IV, with the exception of those made of California and Indiana, approximately one-third of the principals of high schools enrolling more than one hundred and fifty pupils reported having a woman officially appointed to supervise the school life of girls. Some of these women reported as "deans" are in an intermediate or transitional stage between a teacher-adviser and a dean performing the broad functions of the position. If we may judge by the one complete study of a state situation, "full-fledged" deans are probably not appointed at present in more than one-fourth of the high schools having an enrollment of more than one hundred and fifty pupils. The possibilities for expansion in the position are consequently great. Whether or not this expansion takes place depends largely upon the sensitivity of educational administrators to the needs of girls and to social values of education, to the success of deans in service in demonstrating the value of their work, and upon the ability of leaders in the field to build up a body of professional subject matter worthy of their mission, and commensurate with the goals which they have set up.

Title. The title most frequently used and preferred is that of "Dean of Girls." In some states, however, the titles of "Adviser of Girls" and "Vice-Principal" are more common. If the title of "Dean of Girls" were generally accepted and used to connote a definite status and function, the present lack of standardization in regard to salary, rank, relationships to other members of the staff, and major duties of the dean's office would tend to be corrected.

Salary. In individual cases, salary at present does not seem to be commensurate with experience and training. There are many other factors which may influence salary in a particular case, such as size of city, size of school, general salary schedules, length of service in the school, and rank in the school. The only generalization concerning salary which can be made is that, since the salary of half of these deans falls between $2,218 and $3,200, and since these deans seem to be representative of the country in this respect, there is an even chance that the salary of a given dean will fall between these limits.

It is quite evident from this study that the dean who will really make desirable changes in the lives of girls must possess natural leadership qualities of a superior type. More than that, she is a specialist, and, like other specialists, must pass through a long period of preparation. Inevitably in time the law of supply and demand will operate to pay such a woman a salary which recognizes the relative scarcity of genius in leadership, and is commensurate with her long years of training. Probably the present relatively small salaries are due, in part at least, to lack of understanding of the nature of the dean's work and her necessary qualifications. That the tendency is toward better salaries is indicated by a comparison of salaries of the deans of California as studied by Sturtevant in 1923, by Barker in 1923, and by Good in 1927.

Experience and Training. The hundred selected deans have a background of experience and training that seems to be suitable for high school deans in general, namely, four years of college, teaching experience, administrative experience, graduate study, incidental advisory experience, and travel. The four years of college should give the dean a common cultural background; the teaching experience should give her an insight into the academic problems of the secondary school; the experience as head of department, principal, or assistant principal should aid her in the executive aspects of work; graduate study in the field of advisers of women and girls should increase the dean's knowledge and thus contribute to her skill in performing her duties, and enable her to see the position in its larger relationships; experience as sponsor of clubs, grade adviser, camp director, and the like gives her first-hand knowledge of the management of clubs and of the recreational interests of individual girls; finally, travel adds another broadening influence. A group of women with successful experience and training along these lines will doubtless do much to make the position of dean of girls an influential and strategic one in secondary education.

Duties. It is clear from this study that the duties of the dean are those of a leader in education, and that, as such, she may be expected to have an influence on the development of educational policy and on the working out of educational theory in practical situations. As a member of the faculty who has administrative functions, especially as they are related to the student personnel and group activity program, and more especially to girls, she should be effective in helping to improve at least four aspects of secondary education.

1. The first aspect is the large size of the secondary schools, which results in lack of "opportunities for educative contacts." The dean's work with individual pupils and her conferences with teachers, grade advisers, and sponsors may materially increase these worthwhile contacts. Through the dean's efforts small discussion groups of pupils and teachers, subject matter clubs limited in size and led by teachers genuinely interested in their subjects, and more personal relationships between teachers and pupils, may be established.

2. Though the term "individual differences" should include in

its connotation the individual needs of girls, it has apparently been found advisable to have a woman with administrative and advisory functions on each high school faculty, especially appointed to meet this new emphasis in educational theory as it relates to girls. In conferences with the principal, in faculty meetings, and in committee meetings, the dean with a progressive educational background can influence school policies in regard to the selection and classification of girls, the methods and means of giving them vocational and educational guidance, and the ways of discovering and following up cases of superior or special abilities of girls. In her personal contacts with girls, the dean with the assistance of teachers, advisers, psychologist, nurse, and other special officers may help them to profit by the work which the high school offers. In other words, the dean, through her administrative function, may help in the reorganization of the school to meet the needs of individual pupils and through her personal advisory work may assist them in adjusting themselves to the school.

3. A third problem of secondary education is the lack of unity in the curriculum. In the improvement of this condition also the dean may share. One of the functions of the dean is the educational guidance of individual girls. In such guidance activities as assembly periods, small discussion groups, and orientation courses, the dean can suggest to each girl as far as possible a unified program of studies and point out to her the relationships between the subjects she finally chooses. In her work on committees for curriculum revision, and in conferences with principal and teachers, the dean may emphasize the need for, and sometimes point out means of securing, a more unified high school curriculum.

The successful performance of all these duties relating to the fundamental academic problems of the high school presupposes on the part of the dean a basis of teaching experience in high school and recent graduate study in the field of secondary education.

4. A fourth aspect of high school which demands attention is the social adjustment of pupils. For this phase of high school life the dean in most cases must assume primary responsibility. Through her important conferences with committees of pupils and officers of organizations, through the initiation of new activities as need for them arises, through her attendance at meetings of extra-curriculum activities, through her conferences with sponsors of girls' organizations, the dean may seek to develop leadership, give

opportunities for normal social relationships between adolescent boys and girls, supplement the recreational offerings of the community, and provide practice in the worthy use of leisure.

These are only a few of the larger aspects of secondary education in which the dean may exert a desirable influence. A study of the duties actually performed by those deans show many other needs which are being met by this office.

CHAPTER XI

COMPARISON OF THE POSITION OF DEAN OF GIRLS IN NEW YORK STATE WITH THE POSITION AS REPRESENTED BY ONE HUNDRED SELECTED DEANS

It will be seen that the scope of this report dealing with the dean of girls includes three phases—a study of the percentage in six states of high schools having deans; a study of one hundred deans selected on the basis of certain professional criteria to represent the best practice in the position in the country as a whole; and a study of unselected deans in an entire state.

As part of a larger investigation of the status and function of the dean of girls in high school, the study of the situation in New York State is valuable chiefly because it is a picture of conditions in the schools of a given area. Similar studies made by associations of deans in other states will further enlarge the conception of the dean's position as it has developed under the exigencies of present conditions.

In an investigation of the work of deans who were selected on the basis of professional excellence, it might well be that the composite picture of their salary, rank, methods of appointment, age, preparation, and duties would differ from that of the rank and file of deans in a given area. Salary levels, rank, and quality of preparation might be higher in the former than in the latter group. The average teaching load might be lower.

The findings concerning the work of the hundred deans would show practice and status under the favorable conditions of recognized professional standing, and should point the direction for the development of the profession; those findings concerning the more inclusive group would show the *status quo* of the profession within a given area, and provide a basis of comparison between the two groups.

The primary purpose of this chapter, accordingly, is to compare the status and function of a group of deans in one geographical area with that of a group of one hundred deans selected from various parts of the United States. The geographical area chosen was New York State. Studies, now in progress, of the dean of girls in other states will show whether or not New York State is representative of the work of deans of girls in the country as a whole.

NUMBER OF DEANS OF GIRLS IN NEW YORK STATE

In October, 1928, questionnaires were sent to the principals of all the senior high schools in New York State [1] enrolling one hundred and fifty or more pupils. These questionnaires were devised to obtain information on three points: (1) Whether there is a woman officially appointed in the school to supervise the various phases of school life among all the girls; (2) what her title is; and (3) what her name is. (See questionnaire, Appendix B.) Two hundred and fifty-seven of these questionnaires were sent; all were returned. This one hundred per cent of return makes it possible to know definitely the number of high schools in New York State whose principals report having a woman officially appointed to supervise the various phases of school life among the girls.

It was found, however, that all the women reported as deans by the principals did not conform to this description of the position. Seven deans disclaimed the title when the questionnaire concerning their duties was sent to them. In six other cases the answers to the questionnaires indicated that the position which had been designated as that of dean of girls was in reality only a transition state not far removed from the "teacher-adviser" carrying a full teaching load and doing as much advisory work as time permitted. In three cases, the so-called "dean" was an assistant principal whose administrative or teaching duties occupied the major part of her professional time. In two cases the person reported as "dean" apparently performs only the duties of a school nurse.

Because the dean's position is in a transition stage, the number of high schools in the state having such a position can not be stated precisely. The number of schools whose principals report having a woman officially appointed to supervise the various phases of school life among all the girls is obviously not the same as the

[1] *Twenty-third Annual Report of the Education Department for the School Year Ending July 31, 1926*, Vol. II Statistics, pp. 176-208. Albany: The University of the State of New York, 1927.

number of women actually occupying such a position. The total number of deans reported by principals represents various transition stages between incidental adviser and "full-fledged" dean of girls. Table XVIII makes this situation, already mentioned in Chapter II, more clear.

This table gives the number and per cent of deans reported by the principal, the number and per cent occupying this position as it is broadly defined, the number who appear to be in a transition stage, and the number reported as dean who disclaimed the title.

TABLE XVIII

NUMBER AND PERCENTAGE OF HIGH SCHOOLS IN NEW YORK STATE HAVING DEANS

Total number of questionnaires sent, 257
Total number of questionnaires received, 257

	GROUP I 150–249*		GROUP II 250–499		GROUP III 500–999		GROUP IV 1000 AND OVER		TOTAL (ALL GROUPS)	
	No.	%	No.	%	No.	%	No.	%	No.	%
Number of cases .	96		66		34		61		257	
Principals reporting deans	21	21.9	13	19.7	15	44.1	34	55.7	83	32.3
Principals reporting no deans ...	75	78.1	53	80.3	19	55.9	27	44.3	174	67.7
Deans disclaiming title	4		1		0		2		7	
Number in transition stage	5		2		1		3		11	
Schools having deans	12	12.5	10	15.2	14	41.2	29	47.5	65	25.3
Schools having no deans	84	87.5	56	84.8	20	58.8	32	52.5	192	74.7

* Enrollment, boys and girls.

This table is read as follows: In the 96 schools in Group I (schools enrolling 150-249 pupils) the number of principals reporting having deans is 21, or 21.9 per cent; the number of principals reporting having no deans is 75, or 78.1 per cent; the number of deans disclaiming the title is 4; the number still in a transition stage is 5. The number of schools, therefore, in Group I, which really have deans is 12, or 12.5 per cent; the number having no deans is 84, or 87.5 per cent, etc.

Twenty-six of the women reported as deans did not reply to the questionnaire. None of the twelve women designated by principals as deans in schools enrolling less than 250 pupils, returned the questionnaires sent to them. It is quite possible that many of those who failed to reply are not really functioning as dean of girls. If this is the case, the per cent of high schools in New York State having deans would be less than 25.

Number of Deans Replying

Questionnaires concerning the status and functions of deans (see Questionnaire, Appendix B) were sent to the eighty-three women designated as deans by their principals. Fifty-seven (68 per cent) of these women replied. Eighteen of these, as has already been pointed out, disclaimed the title of dean or indicated on the questionnaire that they could not properly be classed as dean of girls. There were, therefore, thirty-nine deans whose replies furnished the data for this state study. The fact that twenty-six persons nominated as deans by their principals did not reply to the questionnaire is itself significant data.

Size of Schools Represented

Of the thirty-nine schools included in the study, none have an enrollment of fewer than 250 pupils; twenty-three have an enrollment of more than 1,000; 9, an enrollment of more than 5,000 pupils. These extremely large schools make the mean enrollment of the entire group of thirty-nine schools, 2,286. The mean enrollment of the hundred schools in the study reported in the first ten chapters is decidedly smaller, 1,419. If, however, the nine extremely large New York City schools are excluded, the mean enrollment of the remaining schools is reduced to 1,274, an average similar to that of the selected group.

Titles of Deans of Girls in New York State

As in the case of the hundred selected deans, the preferred and most frequently used title is "Dean of Girls." Twenty, or 29.4 per cent, of the sixty-eight deans hold this title. "Adviser of Girls" is the title used in 14, or 20.6 per cent, of the schools. New York State differs from the rest of the country, as represented by the hundred deans, in sometimes giving the title of "Administrative Assistant" to the woman who officially supervises the various aspects of school life for the girls. There are ten administrative assistants in the group of New York State deans, all of whom are in New York City schools enrolling more than one thousand pupils. The title of "Girls' Vice-principal" is held by nine deans in New York State schools.

The women who are called "Deans of Girls" report that this title is satisfactory to them.

Status of Deans of Girls in New York State

The status of the dean is indicated in part by the salary she receives, the rank she holds, and the method of appointment to the position.

Salary. The mean salary of deans in New York State is approximately a thousand dollars more than that of the hundred selected deans. This large average salary is primarily due to thirteen deans in most cases officially called "Administrative Assistants," who receive an annual salary of $5,688. These deans are appointed in city high schools enrolling more than a thousand pupils. If, however, these thirteen cases are excluded, the mean salary of the remaining twenty-six deans in the group is reduced to $2,815.96, a figure similar to the mean ($2,720.80) of the hundred selected deans, only two of whom receive a salary as large as $5,688.

Table XIX shows that the salary increases directly with in-

TABLE XIX

Salary of Deans in Relation to Size of School

(New York State)

	No. of Cases	Lowest	Mean	Highest	
Group I (250–499)* .	6	$2,100	$2,417	$2,900	
Group II (500–999) ..	9	2,200	2,711	3,600	
Group III (1,000 or over; less than 1,000 girls)	9	2,025	3,240	5,688	
Group IV (1,000 or more; more than 1,000 girls)	15	3,000	5,274	5,700	
All groups in New York State	39	2,025	3,774	5,700	S. D. $1,440 Median $3,350
Selected deans in United States	100	1,480	2,721	5,688	S. D. $ 820 Median $2,588

* Enrollment.

crease in size of the school, and that there is a greater deviation in individual salaries in the smaller group of deans in New York State than in the group of one hundred deans distributed throughout the country.

Rank. Regardless of the size of the school, approximately two-thirds of the deans of girls in the New York State study have the rank of assistant principal. The others, with the exception of one who is not differentiated in rank from the teachers, have the status of head of department. The policy in New York State, as in other parts of the country, seems to be to place the dean of girls next to the principal in authority.

Method of Appointment. With only six exceptions, the principals in the thirty-nine schools in the New York State study follow the practice, which is also characteristic of approximately three-fourths of the hundred selected schools, of choosing deans from the faculty. It is likewise the policy in New York State to increase the salary to parallel the new responsibilities of the office. The increase reported in twenty-seven cases ranged from $100 to $1,300; the average increase was $628—a higher average than that found among the hundred selected deans. Table XX shows relationships between salary and some other factors.

Experience and Training of Deans of Girls in New York State

Experience. Deans in New York State have a background of teaching experience similar to that of the one hundred selected deans. They have taught in their present positions from 0 to 25 years, the median being 9 years. The deans in smaller schools have taught in their present positions a larger number of years than those in schools enrolling more than one thousand pupils. In administrative experience, incidental advisory work, and cultural experiences, the New York State deans who reported on these items compare favorably with the hundred selected deans.

Academic and Professional Training. The New York State deans fall below the hundred selected deans in academic and professional training: 80 per cent holding the Bachelor's degree, as compared with 95 per cent of the hundred deans; and 23 per

TABLE XX

RELATIONSHIP OF VARIOUS FACTORS IN THE STATUS OF DEANS

(New York State)

	Group I			Group II			Group III			Group IV			All Groups
	L.	Mean	H.	L.	Mean	H.	L.	Mean	H.	L.	Mean	H.	Mean
No. of years in school	4	15	24	2	13	26	5	11	21	4	13	30	13
No. of years as teacher	4	15	24	2	10	22	0	7	16	0	8	25	9
No. of years as dean	1	6	22	2	6	12	3	5	10	¼	5	15	5
Salary	$2,100	$2,417	$2,900	$2,200	$2,711	$3,600	$2,025	$3,240	$5,688	$3,000	$5,274	$5,700	$3,774
Hours of teaching by dean	6	16	30	0	9	16	0	4	15	0	0.6*	10	6
Hours of teaching by others	17	24	30	20	23	25	25	25	25	22	25	30	24
Salary increase on appointment as dean	$ 100	$ 325	$ 500	$ 100	$ 264	$ 400	$ 150	$ 590	$1,160	$ 200	$1,101	$1,400	$ 628
Degrees													
No degree		0			1			1			0		2
Bachelor's		4			7			7			13		31
Master's		0			3			2			4		9
Number of cases		6			9			9			15		39

cent, the Master's degree, as compared with 38 per cent of the larger group.

In general, the academic preparation of deans is better in the larger than in the smaller schools. For example, none of the six deans in the schools enrolling from 250 to 499 pupils have obtained the Master's degree.

Twenty-one, 54 per cent, of the thirty-nine deans in the New York State study have taken a professional course in advisory work. This percentage is lower than that of the hundred selected deans who might be expected to have secured more academic and professional training than the average dean.

FUNCTIONS OF DEANS OF GIRLS IN NEW YORK STATE

In general, the deans in both groups perform the same major functions, but the emphasis on certain duties is somewhat different.

Duties Most Frequently Reported. The duty mentioned by the largest number of the one hundred deans was that of extending influence with girls through informal contact; the duty reported by all but one of the New York State deans was that of interviewing parents. Both of these duties suggest a constructive type of work. A comparison of the frequency with which specific duties are performed in the two groups may be made by studying pages 34-35. It will be noted that all the duties performed by three-fourths of the one hundred deans are also performed by a majority of deans in New York State. There were only four duties reported by three-fourths of the New York State deans which were not mentioned by as large a proportion of the group of one hundred deans. Three of these were academic duties: interviewing girls who come voluntarily with study problems; discovering cases of dull girls unable to do high school work; and attending assembly periods. The fourth duty was that of discovering cases of girls having difficulty at home.

In both groups, however, there may be noted a significant emphasis upon informal contacts with parents, pupils, and teachers; interviews with girls who come voluntarily to the dean with various kinds of problems; conferences with principals and teachers concerning school policies and the academic work of girls; attendance at conferences of professional people, and reading articles and books relating to the dean's work.

In both groups the personal advisement of girls is generally recognized as a function of the dean of girls. Approximately half of the thirty-nine deans in New York State reported that they interview freshmen early in the year; almost three-fourths of the hundred deans also mentioned this as one of their duties. Study problems, health problems, employment problems come to the attention of the deans in both groups.

The second major part of the dean's work—supervision of group activities of girls—is of course mentioned by the deans in both groups, but in this case also the emphasis on specific duties is distributed differently.

In New York State all the deans, except those in the schools enrolling more than one thousand girls, personally chaperon school affairs. The hundred deans also attend school affairs frequently but less often as the sole chaperon. Approximately two-thirds of the New York State group initiate new activities, regulate girls' participation in activities and have charge of the social calendar. Approximately half of the hundred deans reported these duties. In New York State directing social activities through conferences with student officers and committees and club sponsors is reported by approximately two-thirds of the deans. This work with committees of pupils has the double value of developing leadership among girls and of extending the dean's supervision of extra-curriculum activities beyond the small circle of her personal influence. It seems as though a still larger number of deans in New York State should recognize this duty as one of the important aspects of their work. Sixteen of the thirty-nine New York State schools have "All Girls'" organizations as compared with sixty in the group of one hundred schools. Approximately one-third of the deans in New York State and one-half of the hundred deans supervise the student government association.

The general status of high school sororities in New York State as well as in other parts of the country appears to be one of non-existence or surreptitious existence.

The dean shares in the control of the physical and social aspects of the environment in practically the same way in New York State as in the larger area.

A comparison of the teaching load of deans in the two groups is interesting. The range in number of hours which deans in New York State teach is from 0 to 30; in the group of one hundred deans, from o to 22. The mean number of hours of teaching by deans in New York State is 5.8; in the larger group, 7.4. Twenty-one, or 54 per cent, of the thirty-nine New York State deans do not teach as compared with 36, or 36 per cent, of the hundred deans. From those figures it may be seen that in New York State there is a wider variation in the amount of teaching which deans do, and a larger percentage of deans who do no teaching.

As might be supposed, the dean's teaching load decreases as the size of the school increases. All of the six deans in New York State in the group of schools enrolling from 250 to 500 pupils teach. The smallest number of hours is 6; the largest, 30; the average, 16. Other teachers in those schools teach, on the average, 25 hours. In the nine schools having an enrollment of from 500 to 1,000 pupils the average teaching load is 9 hours. In the nine schools having an enrollment of more than a thousand pupils but less than a thousand girls, the dean taught, on the average, one period a day. Five deans in this group did not teach. In the schools enrolling more than a thousand girls, only one of the fifteen deans did any teaching in addition to her other duties. The policy in these large New York schools seems a reasonable one. A woman who must supervise the interests of a thousand girls or more cannot afford to spend hours of her time in classroom contact with thirty or forty pupils, valuable as this academic contact is. On the other hand, a dean in a smaller school might profit from the contacts and first-hand experience with academic problems which an hour or two a day of classroom work gives.

The dean's indirect part in the control of the intellectual environment in New York State is similar to the part played by the hundred selected deans. In both cases the dean assists the principal and faculty in making policies regarding entrance requirements, curriculum, discipline, pupils' programs and methods of instruction. She also attends faculty meetings and assembly periods. In neither group does the dean assume responsibility in teaching girls how to study, though she may assist teachers in dealing with some of the social and physical aspects of the how-to-study problem.

The situation in regard to the duties relating to the dean's office and to her professional growth, which have been described in Chapter VI, is essentially the same for the New York State deans.

A comparison of duties consuming the largest amount of the dean's total professional day shows certain likenesses and differences between the two groups. In both cases the personal advisement of girls is mentioned by more than 90 per cent of the deans as one of the three duties consuming the largest amount of their time. Committee work with girls is mentioned by approximately 40 per cent of the deans in both groups. Approximately 44 per cent of the New York State deans spend a large part of their time in granting excuses for absence and tardiness. The corresponding per cent of the hundred deans is 36. Administering discipline is reported by approximately 10 per cent of the New York State deans and 4 per cent of the hundred deans, as one of the three duties consuming the largest amount of the dean's time.

The most significant difference is in the amount of time devoted to directing extra-curriculum activities. Thirty-two per cent of the hundred deans reported the supervision of extra-curriculum activities as one of the three duties taking the largest amount of their time; only five, or 13 per cent, of the New York State deans mentioned this activity as one of their most time-consuming duties. In the other duties listed in Table XI, page 40, there are no significant differences between the New York State deans and the selected group of deans.

Since the New York State deans differ so little from the hundred selected deans a separate description of their position seems unnecessary.[2]

The apparent similarity found, in general, between the position of dean of girls in New York State and that represented by one hundred selected deans may be due to any or all of a number of factors. First, the use of the same questionnaire for both groups might have influenced responses to some extent; second, the thirty-nine New York State deans who replied to the questionnaire represent a selected group; third, greater differences would undoubtedly be revealed by a more quantitative study of daily schedules, such as was made of twenty-one deans and reported in Chapter V; and fourth, significant differences of a qualitative nature are not revealed by this study.

Studies of other states may reveal greater deviation from the hundred selected deans in their status, experience and training,

[2] More details concerning the New York State deans may be found in a series of articles in *New York State Education*.

duties and problems. A study of the tables will show that neither the hundred selected deans nor the New York State deans are homogenous groups; that extreme variations in almost every respect is found within each group; and that these individual differences within the group are much greater than the average differences between groups.

What is the significance of this fact? The answer to this question depends upon whether the differences are due to differences in needs and opportunities within each school, or to lack of understanding of the dean's position. Uniformity in compensation, experience, training, and specific duties performed will never be secured, but differences in these and other respects will become less as deans of girls in all parts of the country approach the best present practice and aim to reach a still more adequate definition of the position.

APPENDIX

APPENDIX A

DEANS WHO KEPT DAILY SCHEDULES OF THEIR PROFESSIONAL ACTIVITIES

Dean	High School	Location	Enrollment
Lillian Bowie	Woodward	Cincinnati, Ohio	1,339
Winifred Brill	Washington	East Chicago, Ind.	
Sadie B. Campbell	North	Des Moines, Iowa	1,458
Mary Connett	Athens	Athens, Ohio	721
Jean Cowles	Central	Madison, Wis.	1,422
Lillie Doerflinger	Shorewood	Milwaukee, Wis.	945
E. Beatrice Gibbs	Lansing	Lansing, Mich.	1,847
Elizabeth M. Hause	West Chester	West Chester, Pa.	425
Emma Hulen	Senior	Niagara Falls, N. Y.	1,341
M. Elizabeth Kinnear	Richmond	Richmond, Calif.	804
Alice McInnes	Stockton	Stockton, Calif.	2,410
Elsie Northrup	Burlingame	Burlingame, Calif.	791
Jessie T. Oldt	South Pasadena	South Pasadena, Calif.	876
Sarah Freark Pollard	Lincoln	Des Moines, Iowa	1,488
Olivia Pound	Lincoln	Lincoln, Neb.	1,163
Marjory S. Robertson	Union	Los Gatos, Calif.	369
Ethel Rosenberry	Phoenix	Phoenix, Ariz.	3,071
Orra W. Spivey	Armstrong	Washington, D. C.	1,156
Hildegard S. Sweet	West	Denver, Colo.	1,359
Edna Tacke	New Canaan	New Canaan, Conn.	397
Ella E. Wilson	Franklin	Portland, Ore.	1,792

HIGH SCHOOL DEANS WHO COÖPERATED IN THIS STUDY

LOCATION	SCHOOL	NAME	TITLE	ENROLLMENT		
				TOTAL	BOYS	GIRLS
Alabama						
Mobile	Mobile High School	H. S. Driver	Dean of Girls	2,089	979	1,110
Arizona						
Phoenix	Phoenix Union High School	Ethel Rosenberry	Dean of Girls	3,389	1,702	1,687
California						
Alhambra	Alhambra High School	Effine P. Blount	Girls' Vice-Principal	2,211	1,057	1,154
Burlingame	High School	Elsie Northrup	Dean of Girls	807	375	432
Long Beach	Polytechnic High School	Esther A. Dayman	Dean of Girls	3,043	1,460	1,583
Los Gatos	Union High School	Marjory Robertson	Dean of Girls	349	166	183
Oakland	Fremont High School	Patricia Moorshead	Vice-Principal and Dean of Girls	1,550	781	769
Oakland	University High School	Marion Brown	Vice-Principal and Dean of Girls	1,566	747	819
Pasadena	High School and Junior College	Ida E. Hawes	Dean of Women	2,560	1,260	1,300
Richmond	Richmond High School	M. Elizabeth Kinnear	Dean of Girls	957	440	517
Salinas	Union High School	Helen E. Ward	Vice-Principal and Dean of Girls	575	300	275
San Mateo	San Mateo High School	Jane A. Comings	Vice-Principal and Dean of Girls	594	313	281
South Pasadena	South Pasadena High School	Jessie T. Oldt	Dean of Girls	730	335	395
Stockton	Stockton High School	Alice McInness	Vice-Principal and Dean of Girls	2,224	1,106	1,118

	School	Name	Title			
Colorado						
Denver	East High School	Myrta B. Porter	Dean of Girls	2,029	969	1,060
Denver	Morey Junior High School	Della Campbell	Adviser of Girls	1,480	730	750
Denver	West High School	Hildegard S. Sweet	Dean of Girls	1,286	634	652
Connecticut						
Bridgeport	Bridgeport High School	Marjorie P. Grant	Dean of Girls	1,685	500	1,185
East Hartford	East Hartford High School	Laura L. Mead	Dean of Girls	570	270	300
New Canaan	New Canaan High School	Edna Tacke	Vice-Principal and Dean of Girls	316	167	149
Delaware						
Wilmington	Wilmington High School	Caroline M. Fitzwater	Head of Modern Languages and Adviser of Girls	3,000	1,400	1,600
Florida						
South Jacksonville	Landon High School	Orra M. Eastburn	Dean of Girls	711	327	384
Illinois						
Chicago	Englewood High School	Josephine T. Allin	Dean of Girls	3,600	1,700	1,900
Chicago	Harrison Technical High School	Marinda Miller	Dean of Girls	5,037	2,503	2,534
Cicero	J. Sterling Morton High School	Eunice Prutsman	Dean of Girls	4,371	2,245	2,126
Maywood	Proviso High School	Elizabeth B. Oakes	Dean of Girls	1,926	1,035	891
Springfield	Springfield High School	Blanche Davidson	Dean of Girls	2,600	1,200	1,400
Winnetka	New Trier Township High School	Elizabeth E. Packer	Assistant Superintendent and Dean of Girls	1,707	851	856
Indiana						
Muncie	Central High School	Susan B. Nay	Dean of Girls	1,247	610	637
Richmond	Morton High School	Donna Parke	Dean of Girls	812	370	442
South Bend	Senior High School	Ethel Montgomery	Dean of Girls	1,996	954	1,042

Location	Name	School	Title	Enrollment		
				Total	Boys	Girls
Iowa						
Des Moines	Helen Pritchard	East High School	Girls' Adviser	1,638	753	885
Des Moines	Sadie B. Campbell	North High School	Girls' Adviser	1,458	695	763
Marshalltown	Elva Grace Cooper	Senior High School and Junior College	Dean of Girls	641	304	337
Kansas						
Wichita	Grace H. Hull	Wichita High School	Dean of Girls	2,606	1,229	1,377
Kentucky						
Ashland	Elizabeth M. Roff	Senior High School	Dean of Girls	586	291	295
Maine						
Bangor	Rachel Connor	Bangor High School	Dean	1,246	600	646
Massachusetts						
Brookline	Mary W. Sawyer	High School	Dean of Girls	1,610	800	810
Lowell	Mary E. Tobin	Lowell High School	Student Adviser	2,500	1,200	1,300
Palmer	Annie K. Slaney	Palmer High School	Dean of Girls	316	157	159
Michigan						
Benton Harbor	Mabel P. Heilig	Benton Harbor High School	Dean of Girls	670	320	350
Detroit	Martha L. Ray	Highland Park High School	Girls' Adviser	3,200	1,500	1,700
Flint	Grace L. Pinel	Central High School	Dean of Girls	2,078	1,019	1,059
*East Lansing	Julia L. Fisher	East Lansing High School	Dean of Girls	225	120	105
Lansing	E. Beatrice Gibbs	Lansing Central High School	Counselor of Students and Director of Extra Curricular Activities	1,170	550	620
Minnesota						
Faribault	Ardis Carr	High School	Assistant Principal	780	400	380
Hibbing	Bess McAllister	Hibbing High School	Adviser of Girls	922	380	542
St. Paul	Mary L. Bryant	Central High School	Dean of Girls	1,950	900	1,050

	School	Name	Title			
Missouri						
Clayton	Clayton High School	Sarah Dritt	Dean of Girls	276	146	130
St. Joseph	Central High School	Louise Barthold	Dean of Girls	1,018	449	569
Montana						
Billings	Billings High School	Mabel Huntoon	Dean of Girls	1,100	500	600
Glasgow	Glasgow High School	Frances Martin	Dean of Girls	280	117	163
Missoula	Missoula County High School	Conah Mae Ellis	Dean of Girls	938	438	500
Nebraska						
Crete	Crete High School	Lucy M. Sprague	English Teacher and Dean of Girls	251	116	135
Lincoln	Lincoln High School	Olivia Pound	Assistant Principal	2,174	1,011	1,163
Omaha	North High School	Helen E. Robinson	Dean of Girls	1,151	517	634
New Hampshire						
Concord	Senior High School	Grace L. Ross	Dean of Girls	670	320	350
Lebanon	Lebanon High School	Catherine MacLeod	Dean of Girls	303	148	155
New Jersey						
Elizabeth	Battin High School	Catherine Duffield	Dean of Girls	1,800	900	900
Montclair	The High School	Mary F. Pilcher	Dean of Girls	1,027	482	545
New Brunswick	Senior High School	Freda Wobber	Dean of Girls	923	450	473
Princeton	Princeton High School	Jeanne M. Wright	Director of Extra-Curricular Activities	300	125	175
West Orange	West Orange Senior High School	Josephine Toomey	Counselor of Girls	507	250	257
New York						
Elmira	Southside High School	S. Carolyn Austin	Girls' Adviser	1,280	624	656
Huntington	Huntington High School	Julia E. Reeder	Dean of Girls	600	275	325
Mt. Vernon	Mt. Vernon High School	Grace T. Lewis	Dean	2,248		
New Rochelle	New Rochelle High School	Louise E. Flagg	Dean of Girls	1,109	550	559
New York City	Thos. Jefferson High	Mildred Freygang	Administrative Assistant and Dean	6,200	3,100	3,100

Location	School	Name	Title	Total	Boys	Girls
					Enrollment	
New York City	Washington Irving High School	Mary Hooker Johnson	Administrative Assistant and Dean			5,000
Rochester	Charlotte High School	Margaret R. Miner	Girls' Adviser	577	286	291
North Carolina						
Asheville	Senior High School	Beulah Hoffman	Dean of Girls	900	400	500
Charlotte	Central High School	Normal Connell	Dean of Girls	1,080	520	560
Greensboro	Greensboro High School	Fannie S. Mitchell	Dean of Girls	1,201	548	653
Salisbury	Boyden High School	Aliene Johnson	Dean of Girls	802	417	385
Winston-Salem	Richard Reynolds High School	Anna Lula Dobson	Dean of Girls	1,839	876	963
Ohio						
Athens	Athens High School	Mary Connett	Dean of Girls	720	337	383
Berea	Berea High School	Evangeline Davies	Dean of Girls	607	305	302
Cincinnati	Woodward High School	Lillian Bowie	Student Adviser	1,500	725	775
Cleveland	East High School	Mabel J. Baker	Assistant Principal	1,400	675	725
Gallipolis	Gallia Academy High School	Florence I. Kerr	Dean of Girls	325	150	175
Oklahoma						
Okmulgee	High School	Jean Crosby Hansen	Dean of Girls	1,249	623	626
Tulsa	Central High School	Floy V. Elliott	Assistant Principal and Dean of Girls	3,450	1,862	1,588
Oregon						
Portland	Franklin High School	Ella E. Wilson	Dean of Girls	1,735	560	1,175
Portland	U. S. Grant High School	Elizabeth McGaw	Dean of Girls	2,239	1,000	1,239
Pennsylvania						
Altoona	Altoona High School	E. Marie Lentz	Dean of Girls and Supervisor of Social Studies	2,220	1,100	1,120
Camp Hill	Camp Hill High School	Miriam Beidel	English Teacher and Dean of Girls	250	112	138

Clearfield	Senior High School	S. Ethel Trostle	Dean of Girls	525	225	300
Connellsville	High School	Florence B. Kimball	Associate Principal and Dean of Girls	1,250	600	650
Elkins Park	Cheltenham High School	Margaret MacDonald	Guidance Counselor	887	433	454
Pittsburgh	Fifth Avenue High School	Mary E. Cook	Director of Activities and Adviser of Girls	1,277	674	603
West Chester	West Chester High School	Elizabeth M. Hause	Dean of Girls	425	200	225
Rhode Island						
Auburn	Cranston High School	Vera L. Milliken	Dean of Girls	1,100	500	600
Central Falls	High School	Edith Chaffee	Dean of Girls	762	380	382
South Dakota						
Huron	High School	Agnes R. Buck	Dean of Girls	463	190	273
Texas						
Waxohachie	High School	Ivy Cheatham	Dean of Girls			296
Washington						
Seattle	Franklin High School	Margaret McCarney	Adviser of Girls	1,883	871	1,012
Vancouver	High School	Ruth Whitfield	Girls' Adviser	899	421	478
West Virginia						
Huntington	High School	Irma Workman Holderby	Dean of Girls	1,500	650	850
Wisconsin						
Madison	Central High School	Jean Cowles	Dean of Girls	1,586	722	864
Milwaukee	Shorewood High School	Lillie Doerflinger	Dean of Girls	945	450	495
Superior	High School	Minnie Rasmussen	Dean of Students	1,050	450	600
Wyoming						
*Kemmerer	Senior High School	Myrtle E. Keener	Dean of Girls	162	77	85

* Acknowledgment is made to these two deans whose carefully answered questionnaires were not used because they were the only two from schools enrolling less than 250 pupils.

APPENDIX B

QUESTIONNAIRE TO DEANS OR ADVISERS IN HIGH SCHOOLS
Teachers College, Columbia University, October 1928

I. Name and location of school................... Name of Dean ....
....
✓ II. Number of pupils........ Boys........ Girls........ Number of teachers........

III. Number of years (including 1928) you have been in this school......
as a teacher......; as an officially appointed adviser or dean......

IV. *Official title*..
Is this satisfactory to you?........ If not, what name do you suggest?
....

	CHECK THE RANK IN SCHOOL EQUIVALENT TO YOURS	CHECK THE SALARY MAXIMUMS IN THE SCHOOL		
		Below Yours	Equal to Yours	Above Yours
Asst. Principal				
Department Head				
Teacher				
Nurse				
Secretary				

If none of the above, what is your status?............................

VI. What is your yearly salary?........................... Were you selected from the faculty to become the dean or adviser?........ Was your salary increased to parallel the new responsibilities?.......... By how much?........

VII. What degrees and diplomas do you hold?........................
....

VIII. *Teaching*
    a. How many hours a week do you teach?........
    b. What is the AVERAGE number of hours taught by other teachers of similar subject?........

IX. *Office Hours.* Do you have stated office hours?........ If so, what are they?............... What three kinds of work take the major part of your office hour time?

1. ....
2. ....
3. ....
Is night work necessary?........ If so, approximately how many hours a week?........ Kinds of night work?...............................
....
....

X. *Office Equipment and Location* (check the items which you have). Office near the principal's........ Office far from principal's........ Private office or conference room........ Files........ Telephone........ Typewriter........ Attractive furnishings........ Other equipment which you have..
If you have no office, where do you meet pupils?........................
....
What kinds of equipment would you like to have?.....................
....

XI. *The Dean's Staff*

CHECK IN PROPER COLUMN	FULL TIME	PART TIME	TRAINED	UNTRAINED
Assistant Dean				
Assistant to the Dean				
Secretary				
Specially appointed counselors				
Student help				

If you have assistants, what duties does each perform?..................
XII. *Relationships*
   A. Of the following check (√) as many as describe your relation to the principal:
     1. Consult him frequently about many minor matters.
     2. Consult him frequently about matters of all kinds.
     3. Consult him only on important questions of policy.
     4. Must have his approval of all decisions concerning conduct and scholarship.
     5. Must have his approval of final decisions.
     6. Talk over questions with him about which you want advice.
     7. Your decision is final and the principal is not consulted except in very unusual cases.
     8. Other relations.

   B. Indicate by the appropriate numbers your relation with home-room teachers........, class advisers........, club sponsors........, other other unofficial helpers........
     1. No relationship.
     2. Informal social relationship.

3. Confer with them informally concerning their advisory work.
4. Confer with them regularly and officially concerning their advisory work.
5. Hold a systematic training course for home-room teachers, class advisers, club sponsors.
6. Frequently visit to observe their work.
7. Other relationships.

C. With which outside agencies and individuals do you coöperate and to what extent?

XIII. Beginning with your first year as a student in high school list CONSECUTIVELY your training and experience including your present position. Please do not leave a gap in years. If a year or two were spent at home or in foreign travel, include this also. Please indicate summer session study or significant experience.

Dates		Type of Institution, i.e., High School, Normal School, Etc.	Exact Title in Each Institution i.e. Student Teacher, Principal, Head of English Department, Asst. Dean, Critic Teacher, Etc.	If a Teacher, Subjects Taught	Other Functions Such As Registrar, Faculty Adviser, Club Leader, etc. Which You Performed in Addition to Main Position
From	To				
		High School	*Student*		
	1928				

XIV. The distribution of duties in high schools varies greatly. Some of the duties listed below are performed by practically all deans. Some are performed by only a few. Please indicate in the appropriate column whether you as dean perform the following duties, who else performs each duty, and whether you think the duty should be performed by the dean. A check (X) indicates "yes", a zero (o), "no". Please pass judgment (X or o) in each space. In cases in which a duty is performed by the dean in coöperation with someone else, this is indicated by an X in column 2 and the name of the persons with whom the dean coöperates in column 3.

DUTIES	1. IS THIS DUTY PER-FORMED IN THE SCHOOL?	2. PER-FORMED BY THE DEAN?	3. PER-FORMED BY SOME-ONE ELSE? STATE BY WHOM	4. DO YOU THINK IT SHOULD BE PER-FORMED BY DEAN?	
				Alone	In Co-operation with Others
A. Personal Advisement of Girls					
1. Interview every freshman early in the year					
2. Interview girls who come voluntarily with personal problems of all kinds:					
a. study					
b. health					
c. financial difficulties					
d. home difficulties ..					
e. personal social problems					
f. employment					
g. others					
3. Interview girls referred to dean by other members of the school:					
a. for failure in academic work					
b. for health problems					
c. for absence or tardiness					
(1) in practically all cases					
(2) in exceptional cases only					
d. for misconduct ...					
(1) in practically all cases					
(2) in exceptional cases only					
4. Discover cases of maladjustment:					
a. superior girls doing average or inferior work					

Duties	1. Is This Duty Performed in the School?	2. Performed by the Dean?	3. Performed by Some-One Else? State by Whom	4. Do You Think It Should Be Performed by Dean?	
				Alone	In Co-operation with Others
b. dull girls unable to do high school work					
c. unsocial girls					
d. over-social girls ...					
e. girls having trouble at home					
f. girls below par in health					
g. others					
5. Follow up cases of maladjustment and make case studies:					
a. superior girls doing average or inferior work					
b. dull girls unable to do high school work					
c. unsocial girls					
d. over-social girls ...					
e. girls having trouble at home					
f. girls below par in health					
g. others					
6. Investigate opportunities for employment for girls who need to earn money					
7. Approve conditions under which girls work					
8. Give vocational guidance					
9. Give educational guidance:					
a. help girls make their programs ...					
(1) officially					
(2) unofficially ...					

DUTIES	1. IS THIS DUTY PERFORMED IN THE SCHOOL?	2. PERFORMED BY THE DEAN?	3. PERFORMED BY SOMEONE ELSE? STATE BY WHOM	4. DO YOU THINK IT SHOULD BE PERFORMED BY DEAN?	
				Alone	In Co-operation with Others
10. Assist in placement of girls after graduation .					
11. Administer loans and scholarships					
12. Handle emergency cases of illness					
13. Follow up cases of illness					
14. Supervise girls boarding away from home .					
B. Group Activities of Girls					
1. Acquaint freshmen through group meetings with the buildings, regulations and opportunities of the school					
2. Arrange to have freshmen become acquainted with faculty and fellow pupils					
3. Direct the social life and extra-classroom activities of the girls .					
a. attend meetings of many extra-curriclum activities					
b. assist committees of girls in planning social events					
c. initiate new activities					
d. regulate girls' participation in extraclassroom activities					
e. have charge of social calendar					

DUTIES	1. Is This Duty Performed in the School?	2. Performed by the Dean?	3. Performed by Some-One Else? State by Whom	4. Do You Think It Should Be Performed by Dean?	
				Alone	In Co-operation with Others
f. confer with officers and committees of girls' organizations					
g. confer with sponsor of girls' organizations					
h. personally chaperon school affairs ..					
i. personally supervise the "All girls" organization					
j. personally supervise student government					
k. supervise financial aspects of girls' organizations					
l. entertain girls					
4. Address, or secure speakers to address, groups of girls					
5. Arrange opportunities for girls to engage in social service					
6. Keep in touch with alumnae					
a. systematically					
b. incidentally					
7. Other duties relating to group activities of girls					
8. Are there sororities in your school?......If so, what is your relationship to them? ..					
C. Control of the school environment					

DUTIES	1. Is This Duty Per-Formed in the School?	2. Per-Formed by the Dean?	3. Per-Formed by Some-One Else? State by Whom	4. Do You Think It Should Be Per-Formed by Dean?	
				Alone	In Co-operation with Others
1. Inspect sanitary condition of the school building and refer unsatisfactory conditions to the proper authorities					
2. Supervise social aspects of the environment such as loitering in the halls, conduct in cafeteria, etc.					
3. Supervise health equipment (restroom, first aid material), etc.					
4. Other duties relating to the control of the physical environment					
D. Control of intellectual environment of girls ..					
1. Have charge of a home-room					
2. Assist principal and faculty in policy making regarding entrance requirements, curriculum, discipline, and pupils' programs, methods of instructions, etc.					
3. Talk, or arrange to have others talk, on intellectual growth girls should make while in high school (Orientation Course) .					
4. Confer with principal concerning the selection of faculty					

Duties	1. Is This Duty Performed in the School?	2. Performed by the Dean?	3. Performed by Some-One Else? State by Whom	4. Do You Think It Should Be Performed by Dean?	
				Alone	In Co-operation with Others
5. Make easily available for leisure reading worthwhile magazines and books					
6. Attend faculty meetings					
7. Attend assembly periods					
8. Confer with principal and academic teachers concerning academic work of girls .					
9. Check and change programs during the year					
10. See that pupils are taught how to study .					
11. Other duties relating to academic work of girls					
E. Miscellaneous marginal duties					
1. Extend influence with girls through informal contact					
2. Extend influence with faculty through informal contact					
3. Represent girls of school on occasion ...					
4. Visit homes of students					
5. Interview parents ...					
6. Conduct, organize, or attend parent-teacher association meetings..					
7. Entertain school visitors					
8. Organize social life among the faculty ...					
9. Others					

Duties	1. Performed by the Dean?	2.	3.	4. Do You Think It Should Be Performed by Dean?
F. See that a positive health program is in effective operation				
G. Duties relating to the office itself				
1. Read and answer correspondence				
2. Check absence and tardiness				
a) all				
b) special cases				
3. Organize work of assistants				
4. Perform miscellaneous office duties such as answering telephone, filing				
5. Prepare reports from time to time				
6. Confer with assistants				
7. Maintain contact with the dean's field .				
a. visit other schools .				
b. attend conferences of professional people				
c. take professional course for				
d. read recent articles on personnel work .				
8. Others				
H. Committee work of dean during past year.				
List committees on which you serve, and indicate those on which you are chairman.				

I. Please re-read the list of duties and put a cross (X) in front of the three *detailed* duties which take the largest part of your time.

J. Please list in order the three TYPES of work that take the largest amount of your time (Personal Advisement, Excuses, Committee work with students, etc.)

1. ....
2. ....
3. ....

K. Do you perform the same duties with boys? If not, what contacts, if any, do you have with the boys in the school?

XV. *Knowledge Needed in the Dean's Work*

A. Have you ever taken a professional course in advisory work? If so, where?

B. Which parts of your academic and professional training and professional experience and other life experience have helped you most in your *work as dean?*

C. Have you ever in your work felt the need of some specific knowledge or techniques? If so, please list them.

XVI. *Other Aspects*

A. In what phases of your work do you think you have accomplished most?

B. With what phases of your work do you think you have accomplished least?

C. What specific parts of your work have been, as far as you know, commented on especially favorably by students or faculty?

1. ....
2. ....
3. ....
4. ....
5. ....

D. Do you think of any specific activities of the dean which have been commented on unfavorably by students or faculty?

E. Will you give us an idea of any work which you feel you should and could handle, but of which you do not have charge at present?

F. What do you think are the main professional satisfactions of the position of advisor of girls?

G. What do you think are the main difficulties and problems of the position?

APPENDIX C

TABLE OF DUTIES PERFORMED BY DEANS AND OTHERS

* A. = alone   * O. = with others.

	Performed In School	By Dean		By Some One Else	Should Be Performed by Dean	
		No.	Rank		A.*	O.*
Interview girls who come voluntarily with study problems	100	60	58.5	72	10	76
Inspect sanitary condition of the school	99	65	50.5	67	7	55
Extend influence with girls through informal contact	99	96	1	34	15	45
Supervise social aspects of the environment	98	74	35	83	2	80
Interview girls who come voluntarily with social problems	98	94	4	42	34	53
Supervise health equipment	98	66	47.5	68	7	59
Attend assembly periods ...	98	89	11	34	8	33
Attend faculty meeting	98	94	4	30	11	32
Interview girls who come voluntarily with health problems	97	80	23.5	78	9	71
Interview girls who come voluntarily with home difficulties	97	92	8	48	32	57
Interview girls who come voluntarily with employment difficulties	97	82	20.5	59	22	53
Interview girls referred for health problems	97	78	27	72	8	69
Interview parents	96	93	7	54	12	52
Interview girls referred for failure in academic work .	96	87	14.5	64	13	66
Confer with principal and teachers concerning academic work of girls	96	94	4	25	24	34

	Per-formed In School	By Dean		By Some One Else	Should Be Performed by Dean	
		No.	Rank		A.*	O.*
Interview girls who come voluntarily with financial difficulties	95	88	12.5	49	36	53
Handle emergency cases of illness	95	75	33	60	7	53
Assist committees of girls in planning social events	95	88	12.5	68	11	70
Attend meetings of many extra-curriculum activities	94	87	14.5	54	10	61
Extend influence with faculty through informal contact	94	90	9.5	18	16	35
Read and answer correspondence		94	4		8	0
Attend conferences of professional people		94	4		8	2
Discover cases of girls below par in health	92	77	28.5	65	5	71
Help girls make their programs officially	92	59	61	70	17	46
Personally chaperon school affairs	92	73	37	71	6	67
Assist principal and faculty in policy making	92	85	17	41	7	59
Check and change programs during the year	92	75	33	61	10	52
Discover cases of unsocial girls	91	85	17	47	12	66
Interview girls referred for all cases of misconduct ..	91	43	75.5	59	16	37
Interview girls for absence or tardiness in practically all cases	90	41	79.5	58	14	42
Have charge of social program	90	71	41	46	38	35
Read recent articles on personnel work		90	9.5		8	2
Discover cases of dull girls unable to do high school work	89	73	37	63	5	69
Discover cases of girls having trouble at home	89	82	20.5	49	19	58

	Performed In School	By Dean		By Some One Else	Should Be Performed By Dean	
		No.	Rank		A.*	O.*
Acquaint freshmen through group meetings with buildings, regulations and opportunities of school	89	73	37	62	14	63
Address or secure speakers for groups of girls	89	84	19	35	25	46
Entertain school visitors ...	87	80	23.5	49	6	53
Confer with officers and committees of girls' organizations	88	79	25.5	44	19	48
Discover cases of over-social girls	87	81	22	46	13	64
Confer with sponsors of girls' organizations	86	79	25.5	21	44	20
Supervise financial aspects of girls' organizations ...	85	43	75.5	57	15	35
Direct social life and extra-curriculum activities of girls	85	75	33	55	13	58
Give vocational guidance ..	85	71	41	58	7	68
Take professional course for deans		85	17		7	9
Give educational guidance .	84	72	39	59	2	60
Make easily available worthwhile magazines and books	84	39	81	75	1	53
Initiate new activities	83	76	30.5	45	12	59
Personally supervise student government	82	43	75.5	66	6	48
Follow up cases of illness ..	82	57	63.5	58	10	44
Investigate opportunities for employment	82	61	57	45	21	43
Discover cases of superior girls doing average or inferior work	81	64	53	58	16	66
Assist in placement of girls after graduation	81	50	69.5	53	4	56
See that a positive health program is in effective operation	81	47	72	62	6	56
Visit homes of parents	80	70	43.5	47	8	46
See that pupils are taught how to study	79	41	79.5	67	0	48

	Per- formed In School	By Dean		By Some One Else	Should Be Performed by Dean	
		No.	Rank		A.*	O.*
Arrange to have freshmen become acquainted with faculty and fellow pupils	78	64	53	55	12	62
Interview girls who come voluntarily with personal problems of all kinds	78	76	30.5	32	16	48
Prepare reports from time to time		77	28.5		6	8
Regulate girls' participation in extra-classroom activities	77	67	46	32	21	48
Follow up cases of girls below par in health	77	57	63.5	54	7	59
Have charge of home-room .	77	16	87	64	1	37
Arrange opportunities for girls to engage in social service	76	64	53	42	14	50
Follow up cases of unsocial girls	75	68	45	23	20	54
Keep in touch with alumnae incidentally	75	63	55	37	7	47
Conduct, organize, or attend parent-teacher association meetings.........	73	71	41	30	8	43
Follow up cases of girls having trouble at home	72	66	47.5	28	26	43
Visit other schools		70	43.5		8	0
Interview every freshman early in the year	69	50	69.5	37	23	52
Follow up cases of dull girls unable to do high school work	69	59	61	33	18	49
Follow up cases of over-social girls	69	63	55	23	19	49
Administer loans and scholarships	69	52	68	47	12	55
Interview girls referred for conduct in exceptional cases only	68	65	50.5	34	20	44
Interview girls referred to dean for absence or tardiness in exceptional cases only	66	63	55	28	23	30
Represent girls of school on occasion	66	65	50.5	12	23	21

	PER-FORMED IN SCHOOL	BY DEAN		BY SOME ONE ELSE	SHOULD BE PERFORMED BY DEAN	
		No.	Rank		A.*	O.*
Check absence and tardiness in special cases		65	50.5		6	7
Organize social life among the faculty	62	36	82	44	4	45
Follow up cases of superior girls doing average or inferior work	62	53	66.5	18	16	49
Perform miscellaneous office duties		60	58.5		2	5
Confer with assistants		59	61		6	2
Personally supervise the "All Girls' Organization"	59	53	66.5	18	32	28
Approve conditions under which girls work	59	43	75.5	25	18	33
Unofficially help girls to make their programs	58	49	71	24	5	26
Organize work of assistants .		54	65		6	2
Talk, or arrange to have others talk, on intellectual growth girls should make while in high school (Orientation Course)	52	45	73	19	26	31
Confer with principal concerning the selection of faculty	48	27	86	26	4	28
Entertain girls	42	32	83.5	24	10	29
Check all absence and tardiness		32	83.5		1	7
Supervise girls boarding away from home	31	30	85	4	23	17
Systematically keep in touch with alumnae	16	5	88	13	3	12
83—report no sororities 14—report sororities *Others*						
Other duties relating to control of the physical environment	33	25		21	2	23
Other duties relating to interviewing girls who come voluntarily with personal problems	31	25		11	7	13
Other duties relating to academic work of girls ..	24	20		14	1	15

	Per-formed In School	By Dean		By Some One Else	Should Be Performed by Dean	
		No.	Rank		A.*	O.*
Other cases of maladjustment discovered	18	16		11	0	10
Other cases of maladjustment followed up	14	12		6	3	11
Other duties relating to group activities of girls .	13	11		5	3	4
Other miscellaneous marginal duties	8	7		4	0	5
Other duties relating to the office itself		8			6